ENVIRONMENTAL SCIENCE - CONSERVATION

OUR
NATURAL RESOURCES

JOHN TOMIKEL
ALLEGHENY PRESS

Front Cover Photo: **Red Wolf: When this photo was taken in 1987 there were only 17 Red Wolves in the world. In 1995, there were 276.**

Back Cover Photo: **Sea Oats: Sea oats are found in scattered areas along the beaches of the Atlantic Coast. These were found in North Carolina.**

Title Page Photo: Glacier National Park

Library of Congress Catalog Number: 95-94396

ISBN 0-910042 - 74 - 8

Address all correspondence concerning this work to
Allegheny Press
19323 Elgin Road
Corry PA 16407

CONTENTS

PHOTO CREDITS
(page numbers)
U.S. Dept of Agriculture 8, 21, 22, 33, 44, 46, 95, 98, 99

U.S. Dept of the Interior 19. 26. 27. 28. 60. 62. 76. 107. 118

U.S. Forest Service 50, 51, 57

Dr.Henry Lawrence 25, 29, 31, 55, 97, 113, 114

Pennsylvania Fish Commission 7, 69, 81, 84

Pennsylvania Game Commission 63, 68

Cutter Insect Repellent 108, Caterpillar Company 111   WaterAir of England 116
Phillipine Tourist Bureau 36, RIA Novosti 11, Chris Nelson 13

Cover Photos and all others by the author.

The author extends his appreciation to Dr. Henry Lawrence and Carol Baker for their
assistence in preparing the manuscript for publication.

John Tomikel
Edinboro University

1. NATURAL RESOURCES

A natural resource is any thing obtained from the earth that is used by humans to satisfy needs or wants. Conservation is the wise and cautious use of the resource.

The human population is increasing so rapidly that it can safely be said we are running out of resources. Countries like the United States use more than their share of resources. The United States has about five percent of the world's population and uses about one third of the world resources consumed each year. We use eleven times the world average energy, six times the steel and four times the grain. Even small population increases in the United States has repercussions around the world.

If we tried to raise the world standard of living to the level of the United States it would be an impossible task. In order to equalize the world resources we would have to decrease our consumption by more than seven hundred percent. We, of course, are not likely to do that.

Resources can be divided into renewable and nonrenewable. Forests and rangelands are renewable resources. Minerals are not renewable, once gone, they will be gone forever. Although resources such as soil are renewable, it takes such a long time to build a soil that they are considered almost nonrenewable.

We can conserve the nonrenewable resources by recycling, reclamation and substitution but eventually we will run out of them. Even the renewable resources might be in danger since we are not practicing sustainable management. We should be cutting our forests at the rate of forest growth but we are cutting the forests at a greater rate than that of growth. As a result, many places on earth where forests once flourished are now denuded. The environmental consequences of this have been dramatic.

America has been named the "throwaway society". We use resources at a tremendous rate and put them into landfills or pollute the earth with them. We should adopt a philosophy of a sustainable society where our use of resources is limited to the availability and conservation of those resources. This would require sacrifice on our part and a definite reduction in our throwaway mentality.

The conservation movement in the United States started about a hundred years ago (1908) when President Theodore Roosevelt and his Secretary of the Interior Gifford Pinchot invited civic and scientific leaders to form a National Conservation Commission. This resulted in the first Natural Resource Inventory and set up conservation agencies in

1-1 The last bison in the wild was shot in 1894. About two hundred were left in wayside zoos and on some farms. The American Bison Society, formed in 1905, saved the bison from extinction. Today, there are about 150,000 bison, most of them in private herds.

all the states. Prior to this meeting Congress had passed the Federal Forest Reserves Act (1891) which was an attempt to put federal forests off-limits to development and the Lacey Act (1900) which made it illegal to transport wildlife across state borders.

During the years of the Great Depression when a large number of Americans were unemployed, President Franklin D. Roosevelt began to rebuild America and give employment to individuals with such programs as the Civilian Conservation Corps which constructed bridges, built roads and started flood and fire control programs in our forests. The Soil Conservation Service was established in 1935. It dealt with the soil erosion and conservation involved with dust storms of the Great Plains. Other projects during this time period included the creation of the Works Progress Administration which worked on roads and city infrastructure. One of the biggest accomplishments was the North American Wildlife and Resource Conference of 1936. It started a tradition which lasts to the present day.

World War II (1941-1945) took the country's mind off conservation and many practices were put on hold as the country exploited its soils and minerals in the war effort. The country was in a state of catching-up after the war. This war mind-set lasted into the 1950s.

The modern environmental movement can be said to have started with the publication of Rachel Carson's book *Silent Spring* in 1962. It detailed how the use of pesticides was poisoning the earth. The public became involved when the book brought out the fact that we were not only poisoning the earth but ourselves as well.

After publication of *Silent Spring* the influence of industry and its military colleagues over Congress was, if not broken, at least weakened. Environmental concerns swept the nation. New legislation

included the Wilderness Act 1964, Clean Air Act 1965, Solid Waste Disposal Act 1966, Species Conservation Act 1966, Wild and Scenic River Act 1968 and National Environmental Policy Act 1969. We became a nation of environmentally concerned citizens.

The environmental concern of the country brought forth the Noise Control Act 1972, Ocean Dumping Act 1972, Federal Insecticide, Fungicide and Rodenticide Control Act 1972, Federal Water Pollution Control Act 1972, Marine Protection, Research and Sanctuaries Act 1972, National Coastal Zone Management Act 1972, Endangered Species Act 1973, Clean Water Act 1973, Forest Reserves Management Act 1974, Safe Drinking Water Act 1974, Toxic Substances Control Act 1976, Federal Land Policy Management Act 1976, Second Clean Air Act 1977, Surface Mining Control and Reclamation Act 1977 and the Endangered American Wilderness Act 1978.

Ninety-five percent of all the scientists that have ever lived are alive today. This has great promise for the future since science is dedicated to understanding our earth and improving our lives.

Scientists today support the ecological approach to resource management. Ecology is the study of the relationships between organisms in the environment. The philosophy behind the ecological approach states that humans cannot damage one part of the environment without harming other parts of it. Each species has its ecological niche, that is, a place where it fits into the ecosystem (contraction for ecological system). The populations of all species living and interacting in an area at a point in time is a community.

The ecological approach to resources takes into consideration the impact of an activity on the total plant and animal community in that environmental area. With this in mind when we build a dam we take into consideration not only its economic uses but also its uses in

1-2 The Wilderness Protection Act of 1964 allows federal protection of undeveloped public land "for the use and enjoyment of the American people in such a manner as will leave them unimpaired for future use". This scene is in the Allegheny National Forest where this stretch of the Allegheny River and three islands are protected. It is one of the few sites east of the Mississippi River protected by the Act.

water and soil conservation, its recreational uses and its impact on life forms that will be destroyed and enhanced by the construction of the dam. We now look at a forest, not only as a source of timber, but as a source of beauty, flood control, erosion control, recreational area and the habitat of wildlife.

If an environment is left alone an ecological system will develop where all the plants and animals will exist in a state of balance. They might get out of balance for a time but eventually the system will return to a state of equilibrium. When humans have interferred with the equilibrium we have had to deal with the unbalanced system and found that it was not in our best interests to leave a system out of balance.

In nature, everything seems to flow in cycles. the hydrologic cycle rains on earth which flows into the ocean which evaporates to form clouds and eventually returns to earth as rain or snow. In the nitrogen cycle, plants take nitrogen from the air, improves the soil with it and eventually the nitrogen goes back to the air. There are also carbon and phosphorous cycles. There is even a rock cycle. Since these are cycles it cannot be stated accurately where the beginning point is on the cycle wheel.

Closely related to the ecological approach in the study of conservation is the concept of biome. The biome is a large terrestrial community that is easily recognized by its peculiar plant and animal associations. Thus

1-3 Motorcycle races such as this one in the desert near the California-Nevada border destroys the fragile environment beyond repair.

we have biomes of tundra, coniferous forest, deciduous forest, rainforest, grassland, savanna and desert. Each of these has its own conditions of soil development and association with a particular climate,

Communities of plants and animals are always in a state of change. They move through a series of successions. For instance a grassy area such as a golf course in northeastern United States will eventually, if left alone, grow into small shrubs and then into trees and a climax forest. As the changes take place, the plants and animals will shift, and populations will change according to the stage of succession. Various successions can be recognized in all phases of human progression.

We are a part of nature, not apart from nature. Where humans have challenged nature, humans have always lost out.

CLASSIFICATION OF NATURAL RESOURCES

Essential Resources
1. human beings
2. air
3. water
4. soil

Renewable Resources
1. animals
2. plants
3. bacteria
4. marine

Nonrenewable Resources
1. metals
2. fossil fuels
3. fertilizers
4. stone

2. AIR RESOURCES

Air is a mixture of gases. We hardly think about air since it is such a crucial part of our existence. If we are deprived of air for more than five minutes we suffer adverse effects such as brain damage.

Lean air, that is clean dry air consists of two major gases, nitrogen (78%) and oxygen (21%). The three major gases of the remaining one percent are water vapor, carbon dioxide and argon. There are also minor amounts, almost traces, of helium, methane, hydrogen, ozone, and a variable amount of human created chemicals.

There are also tiny particles of various kinds that are suspended in air. Most of these are so small they cannot be seen even with an average microscope. These are aerosols and there may be as many as five thousand of these suspended particles per cubic centimeter of air. Atmospheric aerosols include pollen, dust, salt from ocean evaporation and smoke from both natural and human created sources.

The lower portion of the air surrounding the earth is called the troposphere which extends to an altitude of about eleven miles at the equator but diminishes to about eight miles in altitude as one approaches the poles. Almost all of our weather takes place in the troposphere - clouds, winds, precipitation.

Temperature decreases with altitude in the troposphere. The decrease continues to the top of this layer until it begins to level off and slightly reverse itself. This boundary is the tropopause. Above it is the stratosphere.

The stratosphere is often divided into several layers depending on the conditions found there. Mesosphere is the name given to the layer where the temperature begins falling again. Above this is the thermosphere where the temperatures begin rising again.

An important layer of the stratosphere is the ozonosphere, a thin band of ozone circling the earth. In the stratosphere the layer is about twenty miles thick but it must be remembered that the air at this altitude is so thin if this layer was brought down to sea level it would only be as thick as ten sheets of paper. However thin, the ozonosphere protects us from ultraviolet radiation (UV) given off by the sun. This is the radiation that causes sunburn and skin cancer (malignant melanoma). UV radiation also causes eye cancers and cateracts. It also has some serious affects on our immune systems. It also damages plant cells that perform photosynthesis, the basis of all life on earth. So the ozone layer is extremely important.

Ozone at ground level is harmful in many ways. It destroys plastic and rubber products. It causes disease by affecting the moisture in the nose, mouth and respiratory tracts.

The ozone layer in the stratosphere is being destroyed by various chemicals created by humans, notably CFCs, chlorofluorocarbons. These are found in refrigerant gases and in certain types of foam plastics.

Above the troposphere we find the ionosphere which is an extension of the thermosphere. When sunlight hits this layer it sometimes creates ionization of the gases. This manifests itself in the formation of visible gases known as the aurora. Also these ionized gases form into layers which deflect radio and television waves back to earth. Until satellites, this bouncing of long waves was the main method of obtaining radio and TV reception.

Air is hottest at the equator where the sun's rays are most direct. It is coldest at the poles. This unequal heating along with the rotation of the earth creates wind patterns and storms over the earth. Generally in the tropics the wind moves toward the equator, in the middle

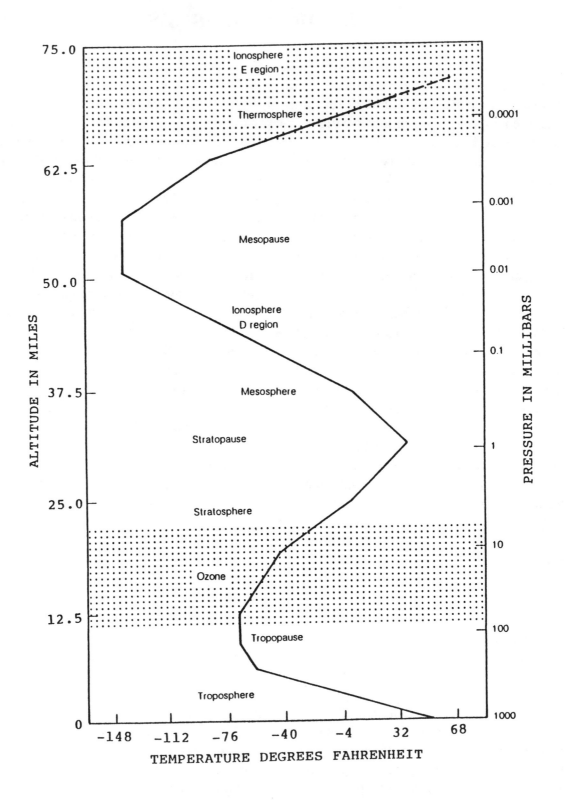

2-1 Temperature and pressure versus altitude in the atmosphere and the names of the various layers of the atmosphere according to NASA.

2-2 Magnitogrosk, Russia - One of the most polluted places on earth. The average lifespan in this city is ten years lower than in the rest of Russia.

latitudes it moves from the southwest and west and at the poles it moves away from the poles.

Air Pollution

Pollution is any change in air, water or soils that affects human health or survival. This definition can be expanded to take in animals and plants but it stands to reason if humans are affected so are other animals as well as plants.

The most prevalent air pollutant is carbon monoxide created mostly by combustion of fuels. Some is added to the atmosphere by volcanic eruptions and earthquakes. Combustion of fuels also produces a wide variety of other pollutants, mostly carbon dioxide which is believed by many scientists to aid in heating of the earth in a process called the Greenhouse Effect. This Effect is believed to be occurring since humans have added tremendous amounts of combustion particles to the atmosphere. However, no firm evidence has yet proved the Greenhose Effect to be a reality.

Sulfur oxides and nitrogen oxides are caused by combustion of fossil fuels, notably by vehicle fuels and burning coal. These are the primary gases responsible for acid rain. Sulfur oxides merge with water vapor to produce sulfurous acid and nitrogen oxides merge with water vapor to produce nitric acid.

Particulates are suspended particles of water or solids that can be seen by the unaided eye. These are mostly smoke and water vapor that is in the process of condensing.

Photochemical pollutants are those that begin as familiar gases such as those produced by automobile emissions but are changed once sunlight acts upon them. Photochemical pollutants include ozone, peroxides, certain hydrocarbons and aldehydes.

Radon is a naturally occurring radioactive gas which is constantly being expelled from the earth. If a house is built along the escape routes then it is possible the house basement can be filled with radioactive radon and pose a serious health hazard. Radon testing kits are readily available to monitor this gas if a homeowner should desire to do so.

Lead and heavy metals are put into the atmosphere by chemical processes and by burning such things as slick magazines. Heavy metals are all carcinogenic, that is, they can cause cancer.

Heat from industrial areas of cities is also considered an outdoor air pollutant. Noise is another form of air pollution and many cities have constructed walls to reflect automobile engine noises away from residential areas.

The major sources of outdoor air pollution are transportation 49%, stationary combustion sources such as electric power plant incinerators and home heating 28%, industry 13%, miscellaneous sources 7% and solid waste disposal 3%.

The major gaseous air pollutants are carbon monoxide 50%, volatile organic compounds 16%, sulfur oxides 16%, and nitrogen oxides 14%. Volatile organic compounds include methane, formeldahyde, chlorofluorocarbons, halons and benzene. There are also secondary by-products in the atmosphere, especially photochemical smog and ozone.

Indoor air pollutants are considered more dangerous to humans than outdoor air pollutants since we spend most of our lives indoors. These include cleaning and polishing materials, formeldahyde leaking from plywood and other construction woods, oven cleaners and cooking odors, cigaret smoke, asbestos fibers, paint fumes, faulty heating systems and deodorants. Some of these can be removed by indoor plants such as spider plants and various species of ivy.

Effects of Air Pollution

Most air pollutants will cause headaches, asthma attacks, coughing, shortness of breath, and nausea. . Prolonged air pollution will cause death.

Carbon monoxide reduces the ability of blood to carry oxygen and this slows down body processes, especially thought processes. CO poisoning starts off as drowsiness, headaches, nausea and eventually a coma and death. It is the interference with thought processes which keeps the victim from realizing what is happening. Some scientists believe that most auto accidents in congested cities are caused by impaired thinking due to excess carbon monoxide buildup during rush hour traffic.

Suspended particles such as those created by cleaning fluids can cause asthma and bronchitis attacks. Long term breathing of these can damage lungs and cause respiratory diseases, cancer and even death. Suspended sulfur oxides increase heart attacks.

Heavy metals and materials in gaseous form such as Polychlorinated biphenals (PCBs), insecticides, dioxins, and other volatile organic compounds lead to reproductive problems and cancers. Many of these directly affect genetic materials creating birth defects and mutations in animals.

The metal lead causes retardation in children. Lead is put into the atmosphere by burning lead containing fuels, paints and magazines with glossy prints. However, the reduction of lead in the atmosphere by restricting it in gasoline has caused a dramatic drop in this pollutant.

The impact of air pollution is most dramatic in forest areas. In the United States we find the forests in the northeast located at the tops of mountains and hills are dying back. The Canadian maple syrup industry has been reduced by 60 percent since 1950. More than seventy percent of the forests of Poland,

2-3 Natural air pollution - the eruption of Mt. St. Helens in the state of Washington. Other natural forms of air pollution include forest and grass fires, dust storms and pollen.

Slovakia, Germany and England have been destroyed by air pollution.

The Clean Air Act

For years there have been air pollution disasters in the world. More than 20,000 people were killed in one pollution crises in London. In 1948 a temperature inversion over the town of Donora on the Monongahela River in Pennsylvania prevented pollutants from steel and chemical industries from escaping into the atmosphere. On the first day of the pollution alert, twenty people died. Before the end of the week, ten percent of the town's population was seeking medical attention. Researchers are still investigating this event and find that all along the Monongahela River Valley deaths and hospital admissions reached abnormal proportions.

For over a hundred years environmentalists have tried to get the United States Congress to enact pollution controlling legislation. They resisted, since congressman are very sensitive to political contributions from industry who argued that this would "cost jobs." In reality, their argument was based on profits.

A great social upheaval occurred in the United States during the late 1960s and early 1970s. The unpopular Viet Nam War was in progress and social and environmental activists were enraged. Rachel Carson published her book *Silent Spring* in 1962 in which she documented the unregulated use of pesticides was not only killing off birds but humans as well. Even today pesticides are the least regulated of all polluting chemicals.

It was short of miraculous that Congress passed the First Clean Air Act in 1972, more

2 -4 A girl in Osaka, Japan wears a face mask. It is not necessarily a sign of pollution since courteous Japanese do not want to spread cold and flu germs and often wear masks. More than half the people in Japan use motor bikes or bicycles as their main method of personal transportation.

than twenty years after the Donora incident and ten years after *Silent Spring*. Until then, Canada was complaining to international organizations of the tremenous amount of pollutants going into their lower Great Lakes region from the industrial valleys of Pennsylvania and Ohio.

The Clean Air Act of 1970 stated that the Environmental Protection Agency will (1) identify pollutants (2) determine how these affect health and the environment (3) identify the sources of pollution, and (4) develop a suitable method for control of the pollution. Levels of pollution are determined by the input amount, space occupied by the pollution and the out-take mechanisms, such as gravity, which remove pollutants.

Human reaction to pollution is based on the threshold level which is a level of pollution below which no harmful effects are observed or in other words a level above which harm occurs. The threshold level depends on time of exposure, concentration of the pollutant and the nature of the pollutant. Radioactive thresholds vary with the type of radiation.

The exposure of a person to pollution is measured in a dose which is the concentration of pollution times the time of exposure. People working with radiation wear a badge which measures the daily dose they receive.

Outdoor chemical air pollution is usually a mixture of pollutants. These often are synergistic which means that one pollutant will increase the harmful effects of another, such as cigaret smoking coupled with asbestos and drugs with alcohol.

Another type of dangerous air pollution

occurs when there is an increase in vehicle exhaust emissions. These gases change their chemical nature when exposed to sunlight. These photochemical changes are always aggravating to eyes, nose, throat and lungs.

Modifications have been made in the original Clean Air Act and the Act of 1990 finally addressed the problem of auto emissions, acid rain producing gases and the prohibition on the manufacture of certain chemicals such as chloroflurocarbons, halons, methyl chloroform and carbon tetrachloride. The pesticide DDT was banned ten years after the publication of *Silent Spring*. Despite clean air regulations urban ozone levels have actually increased since 1970.

There are many more provisions needed in the clean air policies of the United States. We need to have stricter laws concerning municipal trash incinerators. Presently many of these put dioxins, lead and mercury into the atmosphere.

Stricter laws are needed for vehicle exhaust discharges as well as airline pollutants. However, consumers have revolted when faced with the prospect of paying higher prices for less polluting fuels such as gasohol.

Current legislation allows a "credit" system for industries. Nonpolluting industries receive so many credits for their nonpollution. These credits can be transferred to polluting industries in order for them to avoid paying fines and other taxes on their pollution. This system is controversial indeed. Its intent was to keep pollution at a constant level without any appreciable increase.

Somehow, we have to improve air quality on a global scale. However, it is difficult to tell a newly emerging industrial country with limited financial resources that they have to become enivronmental friendly.

In discussing the remedies for cleaning pollution we have to be aware that dispersion of pollution is not the same as cleaning it up. A large smokestack merely sends the pollution on to the next town or the next country.

STATES WITH HIGHEST PER CAPITA AIR POLLUTION.
1. Wyoming
2. North Dakota
3. West Virginia
4. Louisiana
5. Indiana
6. New Mexico
7. Montana
8. Kentucky
9. Alabama
10. Kansas

STATES WITH HIGHEST GREENHOUSE GAS EMISSIONS
1. Texas
2. California
3. Illinois
4. Ohio
5. Pennsylvania
6. New York
7. Indiana
8. Michigan
9. Louisiana
10. Florida

COUNTRIES LEADING IN WORLD GREENHOUSE GAS PRODUCTION
1. United States   18%
2. Russia 13%
3. China 8.5%
4. Japan 6%
5. Germany 4%
6. Brazil 4%
7. India 3.5%

U.S. Cities Leading in Air Pollution
Moderate and Unhealthy Days

City	Days	City	Days
New York	330	El Paso	236
Los Angeles	313	Seattle	229
Phoenix	277	Tucson	228
San Diego	272	St Louis	221
Sacramento	263	Las Vegas	214
Bakersfiled	247	Nashville	197
Pitttsburgh	247	Cleveland	192
Salt Lake City	245	New Haven	202
Fresno	241	Washington	199
Denver	239	Houston	188
Cincinnati	236	Raleigh	187

3. WATER RESOURCES

Fresh water is our life resource. We can only live about a week without it. Our bodies are almost 70 percent water and this needs to be replenished daily in order for us to stay healthy.

Fresh water is needed in many of our daily activities as well as in agriculture and manufacturing. Twenty percent of American food is produced on irrigated lands. It takes over one hundred thousand gallons of fresh water to produce one automobile.

Water is found in the ground, on the surface and in the air. It circulates over the earth in the hydrologic cycle. Water evaporates from the ocean and other water bodies to become water vapor in the air. Water vapor is lighter than any other air molecules and so it rises. As it rises it cools and eventually it rises to a cooling height that causes it to condense as small droplets. We see these in the sky or near the ground as clouds or fog.

Clouds move with the wind and as they rise further in altitude they become concentrated to the point where precipitation occurs. Precipitation may be in the form of rain, snow, sleet or hail.

When precipitation falls to earth it can do three things. It can form streams and run off (fluviation), it can evaporate back to the atmosphere (evaporation) or it can sink into the ground (infiltration). Once it is on the earth it is ready to evaporate and start a new hydrologic cycle.

Water vapor is also added to the air by plants in the process of transpiration. As water evaporates it takes heat from the surrounding atmosphere and this is why plants have a cooling effect.

The hydrologic cycle involves evaporation, condensation, precipitation, fluviation, infiltration and transpiration. As the process goes from solid to liquid to gas, heat is taken on (heat of vaporization) and as the process is reversed heat is given up (heat of fusion).

Most of the water used in the United States comes from surface sources such as lakes, reservoirs and rivers. These depend mostly on surface runoff from drainage basins (watersheds). Because of pollution most surface waters need intense treatment to make them usable for domestic purposes.

Water infiltrating into the earth (groundwater) continues to move downward until it hits an impermeable layer through which it cannot continue its journey. As water builds up in this underground layer it fills in air spaces and voids of rock and soil until the layer is said to be saturated and this is termed the zone of saturation. The upper surface of this zone is called the water table. The saturated zone below the water table is called an aquifer. In order to pump water from this zone the well or pump must be placed below the water table. As water is withdrawn, a depression known as the cone of depression occurs in the water table around the well or pump. This causes more water to flow to that area and the well can continue to function.

The underground area above the water table is known as the zone of aeration since it contains air as well as suspended water particles. Most plants have their roots in this zone and many die when the water table rises and prevents them from ion exchanges between the root hairs and the underground gases.

When the water table meets the ground surface a spring or seep forms. The underground water travels through porous rock or soil. This aquifer depends on permeability and porosity. Simply put, the

3-1 We live in the hydrologic cycle. Here anglers are traveling on the ocean where evaporation creates the clouds above which creates rain which sinks into the ground and runs off to come once again to the ocean where it begins the cycle anew.

hole spaces need to be connected in order for water (or oil or chemical pollutants) to move along.

A water table can be capped by an impermeable layer if its recharge source is elsewhere. If this occurs and the water table is above a drilled well then the water will flow under its own pressure. Such a well is said to be an artesian well.

About one third of the world has adequate fresh water supplies for the next fifty years, another third does not have adequate fresh water to meet today's needs. The other third suffers periods of drought on a regular basis and as their population increases they will be among those with inadequate supplies. The wars of the next century will be fought over water. Egypt has already declared its intention to go to war if Sudan builds

diversion projects on the upper Nile River. This situation can be found in over 150 river drainage basins around the world.

In the United States, the Great Lakes is the biggest reservoir of fresh water. Many demands will be made on this water. Several proposed projects to drain water to other regions have been met with opposition from the Great Lake States and Canada. One project to increase the flow of the Mississippi River during times of drought would drain water from Lake Michigan by way of the Chicago River.

Eastern United States has adequate water for the next fifty years at the present rate of consumption. Exceptions to this are the highlands of North Carolina and the Adirondack Mountains of New York State.

Shortages of water are already felt in the

great area west of the Mississippi River. Severe shortages exist in the area known as the Southwest encompassing Arizona, New Mexico, Nevada, Utah, western Colorado, Wyoming and Southern California with its big metopolitan areas of Los Angeles and San Diego.

It is safe to say that any metropolitan area of more than a million people has a fresh water shortage problem today. New York City must supply 160 billion gallons of clean fresh water to its citizens every day. This is a tremendous task. This water ends up as waste and sewage water and it must be handled and disposed of in a sanitary manner.

Water Pollution

Water is scarce on a third of the earth's surface. Where it is available it is threatened by pollution which makes it difficult to treat and consume. Every major river of the world carries some kind of pollutant to the ocean. Every society that uses water must purify it if it wants to avoid disaster.

The major pollutant in most waters is caused by erosion and agriculture. As farmers till the soil much of it washes into streams and is carried away. This sediment is moved along by the river and it must be removed in order for the water to be used. The Mississippi River carries enough sediment to fill 60 railroad boxcars every hour, 24 hours a day. Sediment is also a product of ranching where overgrazing has bared the soil and exposed it to weather elements.

Along with soil erosion, human and animal wastes and fertilizers contaminate waterways. These cause excess development of nuisance plants such as algae which clouds the water and prevents the growth of beneficial bottom plants (benthic). As the algae dies off it uses dissolved oxygen in the water which causes aquatic animals to die. This process is called eutrophication.

Untreated sewage causes pathogens which are disease bearing bacteria, parasites and viruses, to enter water systems. Pathogens also enter watersheds and streams from livestock and other animal wastes. Around the world about five million people die each year from diseases contracted from drinking water. Diarrhea is the leading cause of infant deaths in the world and almost all of the incidents come from drinking water. Other diseases transmitted by contaminated water include cholera, dysentery, gastroenteritis, hepatitis and typhoid fever.

Chemicals find their way into drinking water from the thousands of industries located around the world. Even the most sophisticated water treatment facilities usually treat for bacteria and have no reasonable way of removing chemicals. One pint of oil will contaminate a million gallons of water making it unfit for drinking.

When we can identify the source of pollution we call that a point source. Usually these involve an industrial operation, coal mine, oil drilling, sewage discharge or a collection ditch or pond. In some instances the pollution comes from a large area such as a farming district and it is not possible to identify a single source. This is referred to as nonpoint source pollution. Nonpoint sources also involve city subdivisions, construction sites and highways.

Agriculture is responsible for sixty percent of stream and lake pollution. This comes in the form of sediments, fertilizers and pesticides. Agriculture produces more water pollution worldwide than any other human activity.

Streams will flush out their load of pollution providing they are not hindered by low water or damming. Lakes on the other hand are very slow to recover from pollution. While the river is flushing out, the cities which rely on it for water must shut down their intake pipes. A large oil spill on the Monongahela River in 1988 was monitored as it flowed into the Ohio and then down the

3-2 Fish kill in the Ohio River. There are over a thousand industries on the Ohio River and pollution from them often ends up in the river. Rivers can flush out their pollutants but municipalities which depend on the river for their water supplies must be eternally vigilant.

Mississippi. The entire trip took three weeks. In another incident the Cuyahoga River of northern Ohio was so polluted with grease and oil in 1969 that it caught fire. Several wooden structures along its shores burned.

Eutrophication of water takes place when excess nutrients are supplied to it. The algae growth, mentioned earlier, shuts down and absorbs the water's natural oxygen recovery systems. This affects the biological oxygen demand (BOD) which is the amount of oxygen needed by aerobic decomposers to break down organic materials. It is also a measure of how much oxygen the pollution removes from water. BOD is different for different materials and involves time, temperature and volume of water.

Besides agriculture, excess nutrients are supplied by sewage treatment, pet wastes and phosphate detergents. Many states have banned the use of phosphate detergents and federal laws are tightening on sewage treatment and discharge.

Excess vegetation growth can be controlled by harvesting with a cutting machine. A modern cutting tool can cut water weeds to a depth of five feet. The cut weeds float to the surface where they can be gathered and taken to a landfill or composted.

Excess vegetation can be controlled by chemicals but these can also kill off beneficial plants. Some systems of oxygen enrichment have been used in several areas. This involves pumping air into the water to avoid oxygen depletion. This is an expensive way to control vegetation growth.

While streams can flush out their pollutants this is almost impossible for groundwater.

19

Almost a third of our domestic water comes from groundwater sources. Usually small municipalities test for coliform bacteria, mainly Escherichia coli (E. coli) but they do little testing for chemicals.

The federal requirements for drinking water states that there should be no coliform bacteria in drinking water and less than 200 colonies of E. coli in a pint of swimming water.

About half of United States groundwater used for domestic drinking water is contaminated with chemicals that are a health threat. Contamination of groundwater from industry is especially high in New Jersey and Long Island. Contamination from agriculture is high in Florida and California where fertilizer and pesticide use is commonplace. The Environmental Protection Agency has discovered pesticides in groundwater in 39 states.

The Clean Water Act

The first clean water act (Federal Water Pollution Control Act) was passed in 1972. The series of Clean Water Acts requires the EPA to set up a nationwide system of water quality. Although it doesn't stop pollution it requires each polluter to provide an environmental impact statement before pollution can progress.

Cities and smaller municipalities are required to have at least secondary sewage treatment facilities and over 500 billion dollars has been spent meeting those requirements. However, most of the large cities have failed to meet final clean water standards. Cities such as New York City, San Diego and most cities along the coast of New Jersey still dump poorly treated sewage into the ocean.

The Safe Drinking Water Act of 1974 establishes maximum contaminant levels for any given pollutant. However, only 85 chemicals have come under regulation standards. There are over six hundred

chemicals still being considered for regulation. Most of these are carcinogenic (cause cancer), toxic or cause disagreeable taste and odor. The Great Lakes is so polluted with some of these chemicals that states put warning notices on their fishing licenses. No one should eat catfish, lake trout, suckers or carp from any of the Great Lakes.

Privately owned wells such as those found in rural areas and trailer parks are not regulated by federal drinking water laws. However, even the regulated water suppliers of our nation have not been adequately monitored. Only six percent of the water law violators were prosecuted in 1994. Some cities were assessed fines of over half a million dollars. Unfortunately, they don't pay these fines and the EPA does nothing about it.

The Sewage Problem

As long as there are humans we will have to deal with human wastes. In the early days of civilization there was no treatment of human waste or sewage. Archeologists have stated that many ancient urban areas were destroyed by their own sewage build-up and the pathogens and diseases associated with it.

In days of old, in cities such as London, sewage was brought into the street for rains to wash away. Small streams were the transporters of raw sewage. In rural areas, much of it was buried or left in the open. Rural out-houses didn't appear in Europe until the late 19th Century.

Even today, large metropolitan areas such as New York City and San Diego dump lightly treated sewage into the ocean. Cities on the Mediterranean Sea such as Athens, Greece, dump more than half of their raw sewage directly into that body of water. Lagos, Nigeria, a city with over eight million inhabitants has no sewer system. More than half the people in the world do not have access to a sewage disposal system.

In most of the Lesser Developed Countries

3-3 A multi-purpose dam at Glen Canyon, Arizona. The reservoir was built to store irrigation and municipal water. It is also used for recreation and to produce electricity. Ten percent of United States electricity is produced by hydropower.

and the Newly Industrialized Nations where there are sewage systems they are of passive design. Sewage is collected into settling ponds and lagoons. Here the air, sunlight and microbes break down the sewage. After a month of settling, many of these municipalities treat the effluent with chlorine or some other chemical before the pond is cleaned. The collected material is usually taken to rural areas and used for fertilizer.

Most municipalities in modern industrial countries have sewage treatment plants. They also require septic tank systems in rural areas.

In modern sewage treatment systems, the human wastes from toilets is moved through pipes to a central collecting point. Here primary treatment, which is a mechanical process, screens out debris such as plastic, sticks and cloth. The other solids settle to

form sludge. The sludge is either gathered and taken to dump sites or is moved on for more treatment.

Secondary sewage treatment involves biological processes. These employ aerobic bacteria which breaks down the sludge. Another process is aeration and trickling. Sewage liquids are sprayed into the air which kills most of the associated bacteria. The falling water then trickles through a thick bed of ash, gravel, sand and rocks.

More advanced treatment depends upon the contaminants in the sewage. Mostly these involve separating heavy metals from the sewage and heavy chlorination. Some cities such as Palo Alto, California have found a wealth of heavy metals in sewage sludge. In their first year of metal recovery, Palo Alto sold the gold and silver from sludge for over

14 million dollars.

In some treatment system, anaerobic bacteria are added to sludge to decompose it. In this system the bacteria produce methane as a byproduct. This biogas can be used to heat buildings and even run vehicles and other equipment.

In many areas dry sludge is incinerated, but this causes air pollution and is especially bad when toxic substances appear in the sludge. If metals and toxins are removed, then burning sludge can be used to produce heat or electricity.

Probably the best solution is to disinfect the sludge and return it to the soil as fertilizer. Untreated sludge can be used as fertilizer in forests or in reclaiming old mine dumps. Usually in these areas there is little danger of groundwater contamination.

Many municipalities in the United States have storm water running into sewage water. When rains and melting snow is high in volume these overflow with raw sewage. This is a major cause of beach pollution.

As the population increases the human waste problem will increase with it. There are ways to handle the wastes in order to preserve our health and the environment but these come at a high price. There are also ways to lower the cost of sewage collection and treatment. Communities will have to seek these out.

Case Study: The Sewage System of a Medium Sized City
ERIE, PENNSYLVANIA - pop. 130,000

The Erie Wastewater Treatment Plant is a secondary treatment plant having the design capacity of 69 million gallons per day. It averages, under normal conditions, between 30 and 40 million gallons per day from the city sewer system which is called the Municipal Flow. The secondary treatment process consists of the biological treatment of wastewater by utilizing many different types of microorganisms in a controlled environment. The treatment is as follows:

3-4 The biological breakdown of organic material takes place in the sludge basin pictured above. The sludge settles out.

1. Grit Screening: The municipal waste first enters the plant and passes through the Bar Screens. These screens remove large rags, pieces of wood and plastic that could damage pumps and tanks. The screened out material is deposited in containers and removed to a sanitary landfill. At this stage, Ferric Chloride is added to the sewage water to precipitate out most of the phosphates that enter into the system.

Flow passes through the Grit Chamber, a large channel in which the velocity of the moving material is reduced sufficiently to deposit heavy inorganic solids but retains the organic material in suspension. The grit is removed by scrapers which travel along the bottom of the chamber. The collected grit is deposited in containers and removed to a sanitary landfill.

2. Primary Treatment: The organic flow of suspended materials is treated with an Anionic Polymer which forms a floc. This makes the larger and heavier solids (sludge) settle out in Primary Settling Tanks. These are long tanks

with flight boards that travel across the top and bottom of the tank. When going across the top the boards remove floating solids such as grease. When returning across the bottom the boards collect the settled solids. All the collected activated sludge is then pumped to a wet well or holding tank for further processing.

3. Secondary Treatment: The combined primary effluents along with the activated sludge are then passed through Aeration Basins. Here the biological breakdown of organic material takes place. The primary effluent provides the food source and the sludge provides microorganisms for this process. The basins have a series of four passes containing a high level of dissolved oxygen which is necessary to sustain life of the aerobic organisms.

4. Final Clarification: The biomass generated in the aeration tanks is settled out in the Final Settling Tanks. The sludges that settle are collected and pumped back to the plant as activated sludge. The effluent from these tanks is then Chlorinated for disinfection purposes and then the treated water is discharged into Lake Erie.

5. Sludge Removal: Not all of the activated sludge is returned to the aeration basins. Some of it is pumped to the Dissolved Air Flotation Units which are sludge thickeners. In these units, charged water, that is highly oxygenated water, and a cationic polymer are mixed with the activated sludge. The sludge forms a floc and the charged water causes it to float to the top of the tank. This thickened sludge is removed and pumped to the Wet Well where it is combined with the sludges from the primary settling tanks to receive further processing.

The sludge from the wet well is pumped to the belt press filters where cationic polymers are added and the sludge is passed through the presses. The resulting filter cake or sludge cake is conveyored to the incinerators for burning at temperatures of 1500 degrees Fahrenheit. The resulting ash is a clay-like substance which is deposed in a sanitary landfill.

APPROXIMATE AMOUNT OF WATER (IN GALLONS) USED IN VARIOUS ACTIVITIES

car wash with hose	80
washing machine	60
ten minute shower	40
bath in tub	35
dishes by hand with water running	30
shaving, water running	20
automatic dishwasher	10
toilet flush	5
brushing teeth with water running	2

STEPS TO TAKE IN SAVING WATER

1. Take short showers.
2. Don't run water while brushing teeth, shaving or washing up.
3. Repair all faucet drips.
4. Don't use the toilet as a wastebasket.
5. Wash only full loads in the automatic washer.
6. Don't use garbage disposals in the sink.
7. Clean sidewalks with a broom instead of a hose.
8. Water lawns and gardens in the early morning or late in the day.

4. SOIL RESOURCES

Humans depend upon soil for survival. Those countries with good soil and water resources prosper and those without do not. Some countries with limited food resources can compensate for this by producing products which can be exchanged for food.

Soil is a mixture of decaying organic matter, mineral particles, living organisms, liquids and gases. It is a complex substance, an identifiable ecosystem.

Just as soils are complex, the creation of soils is a complex process. The development of soil begins with the physical and chemical disintegration of rock. Rock is acted on chemically by naturally slightly acidic rain and atmospheric gases. Heating by the sun and freezing in winter creates physical disintegration. These processes are referred to as weathering.

Chemical weathering changes the composition of the original parent material, and physical weathering makes smaller particles out of big ones. As the particles get smaller, more surface is exposed to chemical weathering. Once biotic life in the form of plants and insects takes hold the weathering and soil formation process is accelerated.

Soils have texture and structure. Texture is the mixture of particle sizes and in soil classification these are sand, silt and clay. The best soil, loam, is a mixture of all three particle sizes. Structure is the way the particles merge. If clay is in layers in the soil then water cannot percolate through it. A layer of sand might let water infiltrate too deep and be unusable to surface plants.

There are many classification systems of soil. Refer to the chart for the present system accepted by most scientists.

An older system based on climate and formation process is still useful in understanding soils and soil formation. Under this system there are three processes of formation. Podzolization is the formation of soils under conditions of cool climates with adequate water. These soils form from disintegration of tree leaves and needles. The soils are acidic in nature and need "sweetening" (treating usually with pulverized and heated limestone) to make them productive. Podzol soils are found in eastern United States from the Great Lakes to the Gulf of Mexico.

Calcification is the process of soil formation created by dry conditions on grasslands. These soils are high in carbonates and need no sweetening. However they are deficient in moisture and irrigation is needed to make them productive. These soils have names such as chernozem (black earth), chestnut (red brown earth) and sierozem (desert). With adequate water these soils are very productive. Most of the world's wheat crop is raised on these soils.

Since moisture is scarce at the surface of the calcified soils the moisture comes to plant roots from below when it is not added above. Eventually the soils develop a crust of minerals on them (caliche) and if the crust continues to develop the soils are not usable. The crust can be flushed away but this takes more water in what is already a water scarce environment.

The third process, laterization takes place in tropical environments where there is a lot of heat and moisture. The only section of the United States with such soils is the Everglades at the tip of Florida. These soils, called laterites, are high in iron and aluminum. Due to high heat and precipitation laterites are easily destroyed once they are exposed to weather.

Soils are studied and identified on the basis of a soil profile which is a cross-section

GENERAL SOIL FORMATION PROCESSES

Podzolization occurs in cool humid climates resulting in acid soils.
Calcification occurs in dry climates resulting in slightly basic soils.
Laterization occurs in the tropics with high temperatures and heavy precipitation.

Podzolization	Calcification	Laterization
podzols (New England)	chernozem (wheat belt)	laterites
gray brown podzols (PA-MD)	chestnut brown (Kan-Neb)	(central America)
red-yellow earths (Deep South)	sierozem (southwest)	
prairie (Illinois)		

of soil from the top of the ground down to the parent material, usually bedrock. The profile is broken into different horizons according to their distinct nature and stage of formation. The horizons originally were named A,B,C and D but refinements in identification have added to this list.

The O (organic) Horizon is the top surface layer of material which consists of old and new vegetation (surface litter). Next in depth is the A Horizon (topsoil) formed in association with decaying organic matter, insects, gases, water and the activity of plant roots. This horizon is usually dark in color. Generally some of the nutrients in this horizon are leached or washed out. This physical removal of particles is called eluviation.

Under the A Horizon is the E (eluviation) Horizon which is a layer of the A Horizon

4-1 Severe erosion of laterite soils of Hawaii. The grass on the mound indicates where the ground level previously existed.

4-2 Land capability classes of the U.S. Department of Agriculture.

from which minerals have been removed by percolating water. This layer consists of sand and silt particles.

The B Horizon (subsoil) is next and consists of larger particles than the A Horizon and it is also an accumulation area for minerals washed out of the above layers. Farmers refer to the accumulation as "hardpan" since it is difficult to dig into. In some areas the hardpan keeps tree roots shallow since it is hard to penetrate and trees are easily blown over by high winds. The deposition of materials from the above horizon is illuviation.

Next down the profile is the C Horizon which is loose unconsolidated materials not reached by plant roots. It is also out of the zone of most surface weathering processes but is affected by physical weathering by cracking from relief of stress as solid rock is brought closer to the surface.

The lower horizon is the R Horizon consisting of parent material. The parent material may be bedrock, beach sand, glacial debris, volcanic lava or some other material freshly deposited by earth processes. This was once called the D Horizon but since "R" is accepted worldwide, soil scientists now use that designation.

The U.S. Department of Agriculture has classified land according to its most effective use and capability. Land suitable for cultivation is labeled I,II,III and IV. Land not suitable for cultivation is classified V,VI, VII and VIII.

Class I land is usually level land with good drainage and highly suitable for agriculture. There are few if any conditions that limit its use for agriculture. Class II is generally flat land with few rises and slight slopes with a slight limitation such as fair drainage. These soils can produce well with some easily applied conservation practices when they are cultivated. Class III is moderately sloped land with fair drainage. This land is best used for pasture rather than tillage but it can be cultivated with constant attendance to conservation practices. Class IV land has more serious limitations on use. It is generally land above valleys, higher flat lands and slopes that make tilling hazardous. Class IV land is best used for pasture or orchards. Where the land is flat it might be used for limited crops, especially hay.

Class V land has shallow soils with steep slopes, rockiness, or wet spots that make agriculture difficult and it should not be used for that purpose. It is generally rough land which can be used for grazing or forestry. Class VI land is rougher than the previous classification and can be used for grazing with limitations or forestry. Best uses of this land, besides pasture, are recreation, water supply or wildlife food and cover. Class VII land has severe limitations due to steep grades and terrain. This could be used for grazing in some instances but it is best left for recreation. Class VIII is definitely not usable for agriculture since it has steep slopes, almost no soil and lacks moisture retaining capacity. It is best left alone.

Soil erosion is the biggest threat to the resource. This is the movement of soil from one place to another. Generally the movement is from the land to a stream and then to larger streams and ultimately the ocean. Once it is in the ocean it does not return.

It takes about 500 years to form an inch of topsoil in mid-latitude temperature zones.. In undisturbed ecosystems soil is formed slightly faster than it is removed and there is an

4-3 Contour plowing and strip cropping are two methods of slowing down soil erosion.

4-4 The newly plowed soil of the Great Plains states was picked up by the wind and carried as far away as the Atlantic Ocean. The area was named The Dust Bowl. This prompted congress to establish the Soil Conservation Service in 1935. This photo was taken in Colorado in 1934.

increase in soil depth. Once we engage in farming, grazing, building, logging and recreational activities the soil becomes loose and is removed by wind and water.

Water removes topsoil in sheets as it moves down a drainage slope (sheet erosion). This eventually runs into little furrows called rills which takes the soil away faster. The rills turn into ravines and huge amounts of soil is carried away (gully erosion).

Streams are continuously eroding their banks and beds. The banks crumble into the stream and unless these are stabilized buildings and farmland are eventually destroyed.

Estimates of future world population state that the population of the world will double by the year 2050 and then level off at about eleven billion people. Today, two thirds of the world goes to bed hungry and half of

these are in desperate need of continuous food supplies. Optimists believe that we can feed the forthcoming population by various heroic techniques. What these people don't seem to understand is that the soil resources of the world are continuously eroding away and by the year 2050, if present erosion trends continue the earth will only support about 3 billion people at most.

Today, the arable land of the world is being diminished by desertification. The process takes place in lands on the fringes of deserts. Usually, these lands will support some people since they receive some precipitation and have thin soils. But as the populations in these lands increase more of the land is put to grazing. Once overgrazing occurs then the land is put to overtilling and when this occurs the land begins to erode with wind picking up dust and infrequent rain washing away the soil. The result, for all practical purposes, is a desert. This also can happen in dry forest areas as a result of overcutting vegetation for cooking fires and building shelters.

Desertification in Africa, south of the Sahara Desert is progressing at the rate of ten miles a year, that's a hundred miles in ten years. Severe desertification is also occurring in eastern Brazil, southern Peru, central Turkey, southwestern United States, southern Argentina, South Africa, southern Russia, western India and several areas of northern Australia.

Salinization is another soil problem. This salt buildup occurs in areas near the ocean and where irrigation is constant.

The United States Department of Agriculture's Natural Resource Conservation Service has many field officers teaching farmers how to save soil by using various techniques. This agency was formerly the Soil Conservation Service.

Contour farming was the biggest innovation made by the Service. By plowing fields in rows across the slope, rather than down, erosion can be reduced by as much as fifty percent. The water works its way slowly down the slope with each furrow taking in the soil removed from that above it. This is called "walking" the water off the land.

Strip cropping also helps stop erosion. This is planting crops such as corn, grasses or beans in strips along the slopes or in the valleys. The grasses will capture the soil eroded from the open field crops.

Terracing has been widely used in the orient on steep hillsides. By building a wall on a hillside and filling behind it with materials and coating it with soil a flat area can be created for planting. The terraces will hold more water and let the water on it move slowly down to the next terrace.

Planting trees and shrubs as windbreaks (shelterbelts) is another soil saving technique.

The windbreak not only keeps soil from blowing away but the reduced wind velocity will reduce the amount of evaporation taking place in a given field.

Many dry farming techniques have been invented. These involve drilling seeds into the ground without plowing, planting between rows of crops with other crops such as alfalfa between rows of corn, and heavy mulching. Mulching is putting vegetable matter over the soil to keep in moisture and retard erosion. A new plow, the chisel plow, will make a furrow about two inches wide. This is easily planted and covered with very little surface disturbance.

Unfortunately we need to use chemical fertilizers to keep up present crop production. These pollute waterways and cause diseases in many countries. Environmentalists are trying to get farmers to switch to organic fertilizers in the form of manure and green

4-5 The Chisel Plow is a tool used in dry farming. It makes a small furrow in the ground. After seeds are dropped in , the furrow is easily covered.

manure. Green manure is plowing a green crop under the soil where it will rot and increase water holding properties.

In many areas of the world, farmers put human sewage on their fields for fertilizer. This "night soil" is potentially dangerous in that much of it contains pathogens. People traveling in Third World countries are advised to wash and cook vegetables thoroughly before consuming them.

Another problem with food production is the heavy use of pesticides for weed and insect control. In countries such as Uzbekistan in Central Asia the use of chemical fertilizers and pesticides has caused tremendous rises in cancer and lung disease. Pesticides are the least regulated of all poison chemicals in every country.

But consider this: insects get one third of all crops planted in Third World countries and fifteen percent of crops planted in the United States. Other pests include fungus, rodents and wild grazing animals. In the United States weeds reduce crop yields by ten percent. Air pollution by ozone decreases American crop yields by another ten percent. Without pesticides these figures would be much higher

Many farmers in the world are switching to a system of pest control known as Integrated Pest Management (IPM). In this system each crop and its pests are evaluated on the basis of ecology. A program is devised using a mix of cultivation and biological and chemical methods. Timing and sequence are important for maximum pest control.

Since it is almost impossible to eradicate all pests the theme of IPM is to reduce the pests to a level of low economic damage. Pesticides are applied only when the pests become a serious threat to the crop.

IPM uses predator bugs such as ladybugs, strip cropping, crop rotation, green manure and genetically engineered crops as well as some other techniques. One of these other techniques is the use of a small vacuum which sucks the harmful insects into a bag where they are subsequently destroyed.

IPM requires expert training and education to be effective and United Nations training teams are busy traveling to all parts of the world to provide this training. If IPM is adopted worldwide there will be a major decrease in pollution from pesticides and fertilizers as well as a reduction in soil erosion.

7TH APPROXIMATION   WORLD SOILS CLASSIFICATION

Name	Location	Some Features
Inceptisols	high latitudes	found on poorly drained permafrost
Spodosols & Histosols	high latitudes	acid, infertile, severly leached
Alfisols	mid-latitudes	good humus, slightly acid
Utisols	subtropical	severe leaching, low in nutrients
Oxisols	tropics	severe leaching, low in nutrients
Mollisols	mid-latitudes	highly fertile, good organic content
Vertisols	tropics and subtropics	wet and dry climates, fairly good humus and nutrients
Aridisols	subtropics to mid-latitudes	fertile soils, need irrigation very productive if tended
Entisols	alluvial basins	good nutrients, fairly fertile
Histosols	wet bogs	wet and swampy, good if drained
Mountain soils	micro-environments	varies with conditions

30

4-6 Sprinklers irrigate a strawberry field in California. More than half of California's farm products receive some irrigation water. California uses more irrigation water than any other state.

IRRIGATION OF CROPLAND

Irrigation of cropland accounts for sixty percent of the water used in the United States and about sixty-five percent worldwide. Almost two-thirds of that water is wasted. Most of this water is supplied by government agencies to farmers at discount prices. If farmers had to pay the true cost of this water then conditions might be different.

Most irrigation systems rely on gravity to carry water into furrows or ditches. More elaborate systems use pumps and various pipe devices to transport and release the water. Irrigation water is subject to evaporation, infiltration beyond crop root depths and runoff.

Various devices can be used to prevent infiltration, at least in the transport ditch, but little can be done to prevent evaporation and this is high considering that most irrigation is practiced in dry climates. Perforated pipes can

be used to deliver water to each plant, thus cutting the loss of this precious fluid. This drip system delivers about eighty percent of the water to the crop and is the most effective method of irrigation. Spray systems can deliver water closer to the ground than sprinkler systems and in these about seventy percent of the water is utilized by the plants.

Worldwide about 120 acres are irrigated for every one thousand persons. This is about 16 percent of cropland and this produces one third of the world crop harvest.

Irrigated acreage peaked at the height of the Green Revolution (1978) and has been decreasing about four percent per year since then. Irrigation has not kept pace with population growth.

Every country in the world has some irrigated cropland. In the United States, California leads all other states in amount

31

4-7 Rolling irrigation system on an alfalfa field in Idaho.

of water used for irrigation, over thirty billion gallons a day. Idaho is second using twenty-one billion gallons a day. However, the irrigated water is sixty-two percent of California's fresh water use while it is ninety-two percent of Idaho's. Refer to the list for other states with more than fifty percent water used for irrigation.

Most of the United States irrigated water is supplied at huge discounts by the federal government. Much of this is used to produce crops that are subsidized in other ways. As a result we are wasting water to produce surplus crops that must be sold at a discount. In the end the American taxpayer loses at both ends.

Much of the existing irrigated land is losing productivity because of waterlogging and salt buildup. When drainage is not adequate the underlying water table rises causing waterlogging in many instances. In dry climates evaporation near the surface leads to an accumulation of salt which can ruin the land.

The salt buildup or salinization affects about one-fourth of United State's irrigated land to some extent. The problem is severe in China, Pakistan, India and Mexico.

Overpumping of groundwater for irrigation is another serious problem in many important crop regions. It is a problem in western United States, northern China, the Middle East and north Africa. It is critical in India's Punjab region which is the major supplier of grain to that undernourished country.

Much of the slowdown in irrigation is due to urban expansion where cities need more water at the expense of farming. As population increases, the situation will become more critical.

Environmental laws are having some effect in slowing irrigation expansion in the United States. California farmers will lose water supplies as a result of a 1992 law requiring much of federal water to be used to restore rivers, fisheries and wetlands. There is also a move to restore environmental integrity to San Francisco Bay.

An excellent example of the water dilemma is the situation in the area of the San Francisco Bay. Here the water resources are stretched to the limit among the needs of cities, agriculture and the need to protect the bay environment as well as the streams emptying into the bay. This region irrigates

4-8 An irrigation ditch in New Mexico. Water is removed from the main ditch by siphoning. Evaporation is extremely high in this system.

200 different crops which make up 45 percent of the nation's fruits and vegetable production. It contains 120 different species of fish and supplies drinking water to 20 million people.

When water is diverted to irrigation and cities, it depletes the estuary of fresh water which increases salt content of the water and salinization of the underground water surrounding the Bay.

In 1995, the Environmental Protection Agency and representatives of the three waterusing groups drafted an agreement which satisfied all concerned. Each group did not get its demands but each group realized that some concessions were necessary for harmony to exist.

The arrangement established limits on how much fresh water would be diverted from the estuary to agriculture and cities and in which seasons. Cities would be affected most in dry years. The agreement is expected to return

commercial and recreation fishing as viable enterprises. Agriculture interests will be affected as city populations continue to increase. There will have to be a continuing monitoring and negotiations of the agreement.

U.S.STATES: IRRIGATION USE AS A PERCENTAGE OF ALL WATER USE

(First no. is percent, second is billions of gallons per day)

Arizona	86 - 6	Nevada	90 - 3
California	62 - 31	New Mexico	86 - 3
Colorado	91 - 12	Oregon	87 - 6
Idaho	92 - 21	South Dakota	68 - 1
Kansas	83 - 5	Utah	83 - 4
Montana	96 - 8	Washington	70 - 5
Nebraska	73 - 7	Wyoming	91 - 6

(calculated on data from *Environmental Almanac 1994)*

5. FOOD RESOURCES

Most scientists will agree that we have the ability to produce enough food to feed the world population. The problems of producing food and getting it to the consumer are many. About 90 million people are on the brink of starvation somewhere in the world while many countries have large surpluses of food and much food is going to waste. It is not simply a matter of distributing the food but many complex problems of politics and self interest exist in food production.

Although humans eat any kind of meat we have found nine animal species to be the easiest and most desirable to raise for food. These are cattle, sheep, goats, hogs, water buffalo, chickens, ducks, geese, and turkeys. In some sections of the world more specialized animal husbandry produces llamas, yaks, horses, reindeer, antelope, rabbits and a host of smaller animals, including dogs.

There may be as many as 70,000 plants with edible parts in the world that are being eaten today. However, many of them are obscure and less than a hundred are regularly eaten by people.

There are only four plants which really feed the world population. These are wheat, rice, corn and potatoes. These are produced in such great quantities that they take up more volume than all the other plant foods combined.

Potatoes are used near to where they are grown and do not enter into international trade to any significant degree. The three cereal crops on the other hand are significantly exported and imported between boundaries.

The biggest world producers of wheat in order are China, Russia, United States, India, France and Canada. However, not all of these are the biggest exporters and even though some of these are the biggest producers they also number among the biggest importers.

The wheat exporting countries (in thousands of metric tons, 1992) were United States 35,300, Canada 24,080, France 20,000, Australia 8,300 and Argentina 6,300. The big importers of wheat were Russia 21,000, China 11,700, Italy 6,340 Japan 6,000 and Egypt 6,000.

Greatest rice producers of the world include China, India, Indonesia, Bangladesh and Thailand. The exporters of rice in thousands of metric tons were Thailand 5,200, United States 2,300, Vietnam 2,000 Pakistan 1,600, China 1,100 and Italy 740. The big importers were Iran 950, Russia 850, Saudi Arabia 550, Brazil 500 and Malaysia 450.

Leading corn producers include United States, China and Brazil. The big exporters in millions of metric tons are United States 43,300, China 10,400, France 7,050, Argentina 6,100 and Hungary 2,100. Big importers are Russia 18,100, Japan 16,400 South Korea 6,650, South Africa 3,600, Netherlands 2,100 and Malaysia Most corn is fed to animals such as hogs and cattle.

Grains, or cereals as they are called, have many advantages as a world food. They have a hard outer coating and are easy to store for long periods of time and they are easy to transport. They can be made into a variety of dishes. For instance, wheat makes bread, pastries, macaroni, spaghetti, pancakes. noodles and breakfast cereals. The chances are you had wheat in at least three different forms yesterday.

The next food crops in order of production are barley, sweet potatoes, cassava, grapes, soybean, oats, sorghum, sugar cane, millet, banana and tomato. Cassava or manioc, and sweet potatoes are major root crops of tropical farms.

Food is produced on small farms in most of the world but in the United States and other rich countries the corporation farm has taken over production. These industrial farms involve large amounts of capital (money). They usually grow only one crop from hybrid seed. Their equipment involves considerable operating and purchasing costs. And, they usually have choice flat land on which to produce the food.

Corporation farms use chemical fertilizers and pesticides in large amounts. They are the biggest users of irrigation. When they have a choice most of them engage in meat production, especially chicken and beef.

The small farmers of the world usually grow enough food for themselves and a few neighbors. They have little money to invest. They own simple equipment and there is much hand labor involved in production of meat and vegetables. They usually plant a variety of crops which feeds them throughout the year.

Some small farmers are subsistence farmers. They just produce enough for survival and when they have a bad year it means death or extreme hardship. Subsistence farmers also engage in hunting and gathering where it is feasible. Most of the farms in the rainforests of the world are subsistent. They are found in central Africa, Amazon River areas and scattered islands in the Pacific Ocean.

A close relative of the subsistent farm is the intensive agriculture farm where hand labor is the key to production. These farmers are tied to the land. They do use fertilizers, mostly animal manure and they do get excellent yields on their small plots. Intensive agriculture is carried on in the northern Andes Mountains of South America, China, India, Burma, Cambodia and Vietnam.

Plantation farming is a form of industrialized agriculture. The plantation grows cash crops usually from trees. These include bananas, coffee and cacao. Pineapples and sugar cane are also grown on plantations. Other non-food plantation crops are rubber, palm oil and cotton.

About thirty years ago scientists embarked on a crusade called the Green Revolution. By concentrating on developing new seed varieties, putting idle land under cultivation, making pesticides and fertilizers more available to poor farmers and harnessing more water sources great strides were made in food production.

Because of the Green Revolution, China was able to feed its population and avoid famine, a historical event in that country. Pakistan and Thailand which were food importers became food exporters. Before the Green Revolution, half of the world population went to bed hungry every night. This number was reduced to one third, despite rapid population growth.

Mistakes during the Green Revolution were many. Fertilizer and pesticide pollution increased to dramatic proportions in some countries. Marginal lands were plowed and these increased soil destruction. Overgrazing occurred on the rangelands. Irrigation excesses caused distress to streams and underground water and increased salinization in coastal and lake areas.

However, the fact remains, the world was able to feed a larger population. Techniques used in the first green revolution have been analyzed and world food organizations are now able to advise poor countries and their farmers on better methods of agriculture and preservation of the land.

MAJOR U.S. USERS OF PESTICIDES

agriculture 74%	government 12%
households 13%	forestry 1%

5-1 Water buffalo are used to plow fields and haul heavy loads in southeast Asia. They are also a major source of meat.

PROBLEMS ASSOCIATED WITH PRODUCTION AND DISTRIBUTION OF FOOD

About seventy percent of the grains produced in the United States is fed to livestock. Worldwide about 40 percent of all grain is fed to livestock, mostly chickens and hogs. It takes about four pounds of grain to make one pound of chicken, eight pounds of grain for one pound of hog and sixteen pounds of grain for one pound of beef. We can feed more of the world population if we fed the grain directly to people and cut out the meat. It takes about 500 pounds of grain a year to keep a person healthy.

Today, seventy percent of all U.S. farmland is used in producing meat. Worldwide the number is thirty two percent. Feeding livestock involves huge amounts of fertilizers and pesticides as well as energy inputs. About forty percent of the world fish catch is used to feed livestock and fertilize crops.

The United States has a surplus of food each year. We get much of that surplus by giving subsidies to corporation farms and to a lesser extent to individual family farms. This permits the corporation to sell the excess to foreign buyers at a cost below that of production. This "dumping" is met with resistance by farmers throughout the world. By subsidizing our farmers we compete unfairly with foreign farmers. As a result many countries have put high import taxes on American farm products. France is one of these. The U.S. retaliated by putting a high import tax on French wines. The French farmers marched on Paris, rioted and burned American flags. The French president went on national TV and reminded the farmers that France has taxes on American farm products and that many American soldiers from two world wars are buried on French soil.

5-2 A rice field in Taiwan. Land here is at a premium and is intensely cultivated.

The U.S. can produce rice cheaper than any other country in the world, even cheaper than lesser developed countries (LDCs). To avoid disaster to its rice farmers Japan refuses to let American rice into the country. Rice farming is heavily subsidized in Japan where consumers pay higher prices for rice but they figure the higher prices are worth it in order to protect their basic farming industry. Japan now permits U.S. apples to be imported. In 1995, large apples from the State of Washington cost four dollars each in Japan. In American stores these cost forty cents each at that time.

Rich countries have erected import taxes and other tariffs on food. Countries like the United States can sell food cheaper than poor farmers in other countries can produce it because of subsidies and mechanization. By selling food in poor countries, local farmers can't compete and they end up buying the cheap imported food.

The same problem exists in humanitarian aid. By giving free food to starving nations we discourage their farmers from raising extra food since they can't sell it because organizations like the United Nations are giving it away. In the end the farmers line up for free food and the agriculture base of the nation is destroyed and the nation is constantly dependent on humanitarian aid.

Many countries subsidize their farmers in order to keep them in rural areas. Most cities of the world are overcrowded and by keeping the rural population earning a living it will slow down the staggering migration from rural to urban areas.

In the 1980s politicians in Nigeria ran for public office with the promise they would impose price ceilings on food. Since urban dwellers outnumber rural dwellers they easily won elective office and price ceilings were imposed. Nigerian farmers could not make a profit at the set prices and simply stopped producing food for city markets. The government had to start importing food from neighboring countries. This caused a heavy drain on the national treasury and taxes were increased. In the end, price ceilings were dropped but the country has not yet recovered from this fiasco.

Simply said, poor countries and poor people do not have money to buy food and rich countries do not want to give the food away. They will sell food to humanitarian

5-3 An irrigated potato field in Idaho. Notice contour plowing. Irrigation accounts for 64 percent of United States water use. Two-thirds of this water is wasted by inefficient systems.

organizations who will distribute the food free of charge but these humanitarian organizations are operating on limited budgets and can't feed everyone in need.

WORLD HUNGER

It is said that there are three types of hunger - hollow hunger where the stomach is empty, hidden hunger where there is food but it doesn't have the right nutrition and hum-drum hunger where the diet consists of the same food every day. About a third of the world suffers from hollow hunger and another third from hidden hunger.

About 45,000 children die each day from hunger related diseases. The main disease killing children is diarrhea which affects children under five years of age.

Hunger and malnutrition kill about sixty million people a year. Undernourished people do not have energy to work and are likely to be affected by disease and this cuts down on productivity.

A diet deficient in vitamin A can result in blindness. A deficiency in B vitamins can cause nerve damage, deficiency in vitamin C can cause scurvy, deficiency in vitamin D can cause rickets. Iron deficient anemia is prevalent in many African women.

Two brutal diseases found in children of poor countries are marasmus, which is a wasting away of the body, and kwashiorkor which makes the child lethargic and causes bloated stomachs. Marasmus causes the child to look old with wide eyes and shriveled skin. Both are caused by diets low in calories and protein. Kwashiorkor is also related to babies being weaned to early and deprived of mother's breast milk, a result of malnutrition of the mother.

Some areas of the world are nightmarish. In about thirty years India will have the largest population of all countries. India still continues to have a high birth rate despite its predicament. The average person of India is too poor to get enough food to meet basic nutrition. As the population soars their farm land suffers erosion, water shortages and lack of fertilizers. Although the cows of India, which are not killed because of religous beliefs, provide plenty of manure which could be used as fertilizer, the manure is used for fuel and the production of methane which is used to produce electricity in rural villages due to the lack of wood and other energy resources. Added to all of this is the fact that much of the irrigated farm land of India has been destroyed by salinization.

Several strategies for increasing food supplies have been advanced. More poor countries can get involved in fish farming and using trash fish by grinding them into fish balls and patties. Non-traditional crops can be grown in lieu of the big four, crops like amaranth, dandelions, winged bean and fruits such as mangos and breadfruits.

People can eat insects. There are many that are eaten regularly around the world. Most are rich in protein but we have to get rid of our prejudices against them.

Population limitation seems to be the key

to a world free from want. Somehow the regions that produce an excess of food should get it to those regions that need food. To solve both of these problems will take extreme international negotiation and cooperation.

FOOD RESOURCE TRENDS

Trends that shape our future are tracked by the Worldwatch Institute. In their publication "Vital Signs,1994" most of the trends are negative. For instance, they note that grain yield per acre has dropped by four percent from the previous year. Although this does not sound like much of a drop, it represents millions of tons. In the last ten years there was a one percent rise in production of grain each year. However, world population growth was one point seven percent (1.7%) which nullified the gains. Eighty percent of the world's people live on grain.

In China wheat production rose to record levels in 1978 when the communist leaders switched its farming to private enterprise. There was an increase in production equaling 85 percent in the next ten years. In the last ten years the increase has been 16 percent but

5-4 Dried and smoked fish hang in a Chinese shop. Most of the world fish catch is flash frozen or sold fresh.

overall the production had doubled since 1978.

Decreasing trends are seen in production of all grain. Grain yields increased during the last twenty years because of increased fertilization and irrigation. Eventually the limit to which fertilizer could boost grain production was reached. Now world grain production is beginning to decline while the population continues to increase.

Irrigation is declining. Much irrigated land has become waterlogged. Salinization has affected 12 percent of all irrigated farm land. Overpumping of ground water has depleted most of this resource. Also much water set aside for irrigation has been diverted to cities where the populations are increasing dramatically.

In California where much of the United States crops are produced, new laws cut back on irrigation water supplies. Water must now be kept in rivers to restore fisheries and wetlands.

Fish farms produced 13 million tons of fish and shellfish in 1991. Aquaculture produced ninety percent of all oysters marketed that year and one fourth of all shrimp. About two thirds of aquaculture involves inland water where carp, tilapia, trout and catfish are raised. The rest is in coastal marine waters where salmon, flounder, clams, oysters, crabs and shrimp are raised.

China produces half the aquaculture products of the world. India is second and Japan third. These countries produce 80 percent of farmed fish and seventy-five percent of all captured seafood.

Fish farming is a lot more involved than throwing fish into a pond and letting them reproduce. A fish farmer has to purchase supplies, equipment, antibiotics, hormones, vaccines, cleaning equipment and oxygenating materials.

In 1993, the world ocean fish catch was estimated at 98 million tons. This was two percent below the high catch of 1989 of one hundred million tons. The 1994 catch came in at 93 million tons. We can expect a decrease in the fish catch for many years to come.

The United Nations Food and Agriculture Organization (FOA) statistics indicate that the 17 major fishing areas of the world have reached their natural limits of reproduction. Nine of these areas are in serious decline.

Since 1990, a few countries have increased their ocean catches, notably Russia and China. However, the coastal habitat of most countries have experienced overfishing, serious pollution and habitat destruction. More than fifty thousand Canadian fishers lost their jobs in 1992 and 1993 due to decreases in fish populations in their traditional waters. Water off the coast of Massachusetts is so polluted the United States banned fishing there. Fishing in polluted waters is a common practice and since the United States has very lax seafood inspection programs we are always in danger of buying contaminated seafood.

To insure fish in the future, quotas will have to be set and enforced. The world per capita catch in 1988 was 43 pounds. In 1994 it was 39 pounds.

The world faces declining seafood catches per person and rising seafood prices. There have been many conflicts over fishing grounds in the past. In 1995, Russian naval vessels forced several Japanese trawlers from fishing in the Sea of Okhotsk, a prime area for pollack, cod and herring. In that same year, the Canadian Coast Guard seized a Spanish fishing vessel found in its coastal waters and brought it into port. Incidents like these will increase in the future.

There is some promise of increasing fish production through genetic engineering. So far, a super carp has been developed. It grows twice as fast as regular carp. And this new fish has been accepted readily by carp consuming people.

6. HUMAN RESOURCES

In 1930 there were 2 billion people on earth. By 1960 the number had risen to 3 billion and by 1975 there were 4 billion. The next billion was added by 1987 and in 1995 we had 5.7 billion. Population experts predict that the world population will increase to 11 billion around the year 2050 and then level off.

The world population is increasing by 260,000 a day, more than a million people are added every four days. If we are to give each of the new babies one glass of milk and a half loaf of bread each day, then it will take 19,000 new cows and 400 new acres planted in wheat. The world is decreasing in those commodities rather than increasing.

Most scientists predict that the increasing population will put a severe strain on earth resources. Poverty levels will rise and standards of living will decrease to miserable levels. However, other scientists believe we can feed this large population through technological advances and standards of living for most of the world will increase rather than decrease. They point to the fact that even though the population has quadrupled in the last century the world is no worse off than it was a hundred years previously. In fact, life spans have increased dramatically for average people in that period of time.

Whether you believe that there are too many people or not, you will have to agree that people are a resource. Other people provide the things you need to live and be comfortable. In most instances, other people provide you with food, clothing and shelter. They provide you with transportation, medical care and recreation. People are a natural resource in every sense of the word.

In 1798 Thomas Malthus published a book in which he stated that the plant world multiplied by arithmetic proportion - 2,4,6,8,10 and the human world by geometric proportion - 2,4,8,16,32. If this continued, humans would outstrip their food supply and there would be warfare, famine and pestilence in dramatic numbers.

Since the time of Malthus there have been famines, wars and pestilence which killed millions of people. However, the population continued to rise as advances in medicine and producing food have kept more people alive. Most scientists agree that the advance in population numbers is mostly due to a decrease in death rates.

Some countries want an increase in population, especially those where old people outnumber young people. For instance, in the United States, the Social Security System which pays out huge sums of money to retired citizens as well as disabled and dependent citizens, needs a steady flow of money in order to keep operating. Unless drastic changes are made in the payout there will not be enough young working people in 20 years in the country to keep the system working.

Most countries would like Zero Population Growth (ZPG) which is the number of births required for a population to continue replacing itself without increase. Worldwide, the rate is 2.1 but in rich countries the number is 2.2 since many women in these countries choose not to have children.

The number 2.1 is the fertility replacement rate. The fertility rate is an estimate of the number of children a woman between the ages of 15 and 44 will have in her lifetime. These rates are calculated on present births per thousand and female populations in a country.

In 1995, the following fertility rates were calculated: Japan 1.6, France 1.8, Sweden 2.1, United States 2.1, China 2.4, Israel 2.7, Pakistan 3.2, India 3.9, Mexico 5.6, Iran 6.1, Kenya 6.4 and Somolia 6.8.

6-1 Hong Kong, the world's most crowded city, has more than 245,000 people per square mile. These apartment buildings often have two families in one room and as many as four families share a bathroom.

Population studies are usually based on the crude birth rate (CBR) which is the number of births in a year based on a population of 1,000. The crude death rate (CDR) is the number of births in a year based on a population of 1,000. The United States CBR is 15 and the CDR is 9. Since the U.S. population is 261 million we multiply the difference in CBR-CDR (6) times 261,000 (not 261 million) and find that the U.S. population is increasing by 1,566,000 persons each year.

If we take the yearly increase per 1,000 (6) and divide it by 10 we get the percent of increase. If we divide that (.6) into 70 we get the years it would take to double our population (117). We divide into 70 since that is the number of years it takes to double an amount if the rate of growth is 1% per year.

However, the increase in birth rate is not the only factor affecting the United States population, there is immigration and emigration, the number of people coming into the country and the number of people leaving the country. In 1994, Mexicans illegally crossed into the U.S. at the rate of one thousand a day. This when added to legal immigration cut the doubling time of the U.S. population to about 50 years (to 522 million in the year 2045).

Pakistan's CBR is 42 and its CDR is 12 for an increase of 30 per one thousand population. Pakistan's population in 1995 was 122 million. This gives Pakistan a natural population increase of 3,660,000 new people a year. Pakistan will double its population in less than 24 years (to 244 million in the year 2019).

If the food supply remains static and the population doubles it does not take much mathematics to calculate that there is only half the amount of food available per person.

The same can be said of land and all other resources of earth.

SELECTED COUNTRIES : POPULATION, CBR, CDR, PER CAPITA INCOME

Country	World Almanac 1994 population (millions)	CBR	CDR	Income Per Capita (U.S. $)
Australia	18	14	7	16,700
Canada	28	14	7	19,600
France	58	12	9	18,900
Germany	81	11	11	17,400
Japan	125	11	7	19,800
United Kingdom	58	13	11	15,900
United States	261	15	9	23,400
Brazil	159	21	9	2,300
Hungary	10	12	13	5,380
Mexico	92	27	5	3,800
Poland	39	13	9	4,400
South Korea	45	16	6	6,500
China	1,190	18	7	360
Bangladesh	125	35	12	200
Egypt	59	32	9	730
Haiti	6	40	19	340
India	920	28	10	270
Indonesia	200	24	9	680
Kenya	28	42	12	320
Nigeria	98	44	12	300
Pakistan	122	42	12	410

Throughout history increases in population have been managed in three basic manners (1) decreasing the number of people (2) increasing the food supply, and (3) limiting population increases by birth control and population planning.

We have decreased the number of people within land areas through emigration, wars and genocide. In Rwanda, Africa in 1994 two different ethnic groups (Hutu and Tutsi) battled each other for four months for control of the land. When fighting ceased over a million people had been slain. This reduced the Rwanda population by 12 percent.

As you read this page, there are over one hundred wars being fought somewhere in the world. The basic situation is a majority ethnic group trying to force a minority ethnic group to give up some of its land or resources. The resistance of the minority to do this leads to armed conflicts. When a minority group can break away from the majority it usually applies for admission as a country to the United Nations. If present trends continue the United Nations will double its membership in the next 50 years.

Attempts to increase the food supply have met with success until recently. In 1995, world food production decreased dramatically from 1990. Grain, vegetable, meat, fruit and seafood production decreased by millions of tons in each category. World relief organizations simply could not deliver enough food to the starving people of the world.

Limiting population by birth control seems to be the preferred method of most countries. Sterilization is the most widely practiced form of birth control in the U.S. and in the world. In men the procedure is vasectomy and in women it is tubal ligation.

Contraception is the preferred method of birth control for many who may want to have children at a later date. This falls under two categories: physical and chemical contraception. With physical methods of contraception the sperm is prevented from reaching the egg by such items as inter-uterine devices, condoms, diaphragms and cervical caps. With chemical contraception, sperm is killed or a woman is prevented from ovulating. This method uses items such as the pill, spermicidal creams, skin implants, vaginal foams and steroids.

At the U.N. Cairo Conference on Population (1994) discussions of birth control took place. Many plans were discussed. The

6-2 Urban growth consumes valuable farmland. As the need for food has grown, the capacity to produce it has diminished.

Roman Catholic Church and many Islamic nations objected to much of the discussion focusing on family planning and rights of women.

The Roman Catholic Church believes in only the natural rhythm method of family planning. That is, no artificial means of preventing the sperm from reaching the egg is acceptable. If the couple involved does not want to have children they calculate fertile periods by watching the menstruation dates of the woman. Halfway between these dates is the fertile period, usually 13 days after a woman begins menstruation. American Catholics, as a group, generally practice non-approved forms of birth control.

At the Cairo Conference statistics were distributed indicating the use of contraception by women in various countries. Some of these were (in percent) France 80, Sweden 78, South Korea 77, U.S. 74, China 71, Thailand 66, Japan 64, Peru 59, Mexico 53, Egypt 47, India 45, Zimbabwe 43, Chile 43, Kenya 33, Iran 23, Pakistan 12. Researchers concluded that more women would use contraceptives if they were available.

Scientists measure the population-land ratio by carrying capacity which is the maximum number of individuals of any species that can be supported over a long term by an ecosystem. Once the carrying capacity is reached, countries should try to attain zero population growth. This is a theoretical goal rather than a realistic one. Infinite growth in a finite system is impossible. Each day we get closer to the absolute limits of growth.

There are many reasons couples have large families. One very strong reason is cultural acceptability. People in many cultures have become used to large families. They continue to support this culture dictate even

44

though the connection between poverty and population is evident to them.

More children are born to cultures where there is a lack of reliable contraception or contraception is not available. More than 90 percent of the women of Nigeria said they would use contraception if it were available.

In many cultures, men consider it unmanly to use condoms and the pressure to use birth control is shifted to women. This is particularly true in Latin America and Africa.

The more education parents have, the less likely they are to have large families. Education also influences family income and those who have less children in a given society are better off financially.

Children in the work force is another factor in lesser developed countries. In countries such as Indonesia, Malaysia and Burma girls as young as twelve years old are employed in clothing factories. They are literally slaves in our modern world. Boys and girls as young as ten years old are employed in rug weaving enterprises in many central Asian countries.

As people migrate to urban areas they tend to have fewer children. Back on the farm more children are an asset, in the city they are liabilities. On the farm they can feed chickens, tend crops and bring in the cows. Older people also have something to do on the farm whereas these two groups are usually unemployed in cities.

The cost of educating and raising a child also enters into family planning. Malthus believed that people should never have children unless they can prove that they can support them. It takes about five thousand dollars to raise a child for the first year in the United States. Throw-away diapers alone costs $700 the first year.

Education in many areas such as Latin America is considered necessary and many parents make unbelievable sacrifices to send their children to elementary school. In Africa, more than eighty percent of women never attend school. At the Cairo Conference mentioned previously, the status of women in the world was given high priority. If women are employed and educated they will have fewer children.

Infant mortality rates have decreased worldwide but many cultures continue to have the same number of children per family unit. Seventy years ago it was common for one out of three children in lesser developed countries to die before the age of ten. People in these regions tried to have many children in hopes that some of them will make it to adulthood. As adults they would help to support their aging parents. Even though infant mortality has declined, some people seem to feel that it is still necessary to have large families. Some countries have reversed this trend. In 1965 the average woman in Thailand had 6.3 children. In 1987, the number had dropped to 2.2 Significant drops in fertility have occurred in China, Cuba, Indonesia and Tunisia.

Average marriage age has some influence on family size. This is assuming women do not have children before they marry. This is not the situation in the United States. In most countries marrying at a young age produces more children per family and marrying at a later time produces fewer children.

The average age for a women to marry in Ireland is 26 and a man is 32. In the United States it is 23 for women and 26 for men. In China, the government has recommended the Rule of 52. A man and woman contemplating marriage should have a combined age of 52 or more. China gives many incentives to couples that have only one child. They get first choice of government jobs, housing and food. This one child policy has led to the killing of many girl babies since Chinese men consider it unmanly not to have a son. The Chinese government has started executing

6-3 Parking lots and shopping malls prevent precipitation from sinking into the earth and adding to the underground water reserves. This overloads streams with rapid runoff carrying pollutants, causing flooding and soil erosion.

parents who kill their newborn daughters and this has alleviated infanticide.

Abortion is another method of limiting populations. Abortion occurs when a pregnancy is terminated before coming to term and the fetus is killed. There were 138,000 abortions a day worldwide in 1994. These were mostly in Lesser Developed Countries formerly called Third World Countries.

Family planning would eliminate the need for most abortions. In many countries such as most of those in Latin America, abortion is not legal. However, the abortion rate in many Latin American countries is higher than in places where abortion is legal.

The United States Supreme Court ruled that during the first three months of pregnancy abortion cannot be prevented by states. About one and a half million legal abortions are performed in the United States each year.

About twenty percent of Americans believe abortions should be illegal. The confrontation between abortion proponents (Pro Choice) and abortion foes (Pro Life) has caused much hardship for both sides. The situation is heading toward a serious climax with Pro Life forces beginning to use terroristic tactics to shut down abortion clinics. There are about two thousand such clinics in the United States.

MIGRATION OF PEOPLE

When conditions deteriorate for people they usually look about for more opportunity elsewhere. They migrate to other countries if they can be accepted. Many people migrate to these countries whether they are accepted or not. Recent history has seen thousands of people from Latin America and Asia crossing the United States border illegally. Many people consider legal immigration as well as illegal immigration the biggest threat to the future of the United States.

Only a handful of countries will accept immigrants. Most countries are very protective of their borders. Some set up military units to either kill or frighten illegal immigration.

In 1995, there were about 19 million refugees fleeing their homelands in search of another place to live. Most of these were the result of wars. About half the population of Afghanistan was displaced by the civil war and almost all have moved to Iran and Pakistan, countries which are tolerating them but expect them to move back to Afghanistan as soon as possible .

Refugees are people who flee their country because of fear of political, religious or ethnic persecution or war. Today there are about 4 million refugees in Europe, one million in Latin America and 6 million in Middle Asia.

The big movement of people however, has been from rural areas to cities. Cities around the world are growing at an accelerated rate as people leave the land to seek a better life in cities, usually the capital cities of their country.

Migration to cities has led to the development known as the supercity or megacity. This is a city with a population of over ten million. Consider what it takes to get water, food, housing, clothing, medical care, trash pick-up, sewage disposal and electricity to such a place. It is mind boggling.

Cities are population clusters of continuous built-up areas with the city boundary as the core. In this definition New York City would enter into New Jersey.

In the year 2000, the following cities are expected to have the following populations in millions:

Tokyo-Yokohama	30	Tehran	13
Mexico City	28	Buenos Aires	13
Sao Paulo	26	Cairo	13
Seoul	22	Jakarta	13
New York	15	Lagos	13
Bombay	15	Manila	13
Osaka	14	Delhi	12
Calcutta	14	Karachi	11
Rio de Janeiro	14	Los Angeles	11
		Moscow	11

People migrate to cities for many reasons including employment, housing, medical care and social programs. In their villages these may not be available.

If the city does not readily accept the newcomers they move into shantytowns on the outskirts of the city. One half of Mexico City's population lives in cardboard and tin shacks hastily constructed along with pieces of plastic and packing crates. On the outskirts of Manila in the Philippines three thousand people live on a garbage dump.

These shantytowns or slums have no sewage, no trash pick-up, no running water, no electricty and no police protection. People here live in fear of the day when the city decides it no longer can tolerate them. When these people do get jobs they are at low wages and often hazardous to health. People who get these jobs find themselves trapped. They make enough money to live on and they can't risk going back to their villages where conditions are even worse.

A nation can alleviate migration to the city from rural areas by offering social services such as schools and immunization services in rural areas. Building new factories in rural settings will not only employ rural people but decrease pollution in the city.

The definition of a city has expanded from just that of its political boundaries to that of metropolitan area where everyone on the outskirts of the city are dependent upon the city for services and employment. Some geographers argue that the area from Boston to Washington D.C. is one city separated by green belts. This continuation of urbanization has been given names such as Megalopolis and Bosnywash.

Future Considerations

The United States does not have an official population policy. Should a nation have such a policy? One can see official posters in China advocating one child and in India two children. Even though we do not have an official policy we affect the population conditions in other countries by giving foreign aid, food relief and settlement of refugees.

We have legislation in the United States which to some extent promotes certain policies affecting population. For instance, we give tax exemptions for dependents of the taxpayer. This encourages larger families.

We subsidize construction of roads, sewer lines, water lines and airports which encourages excess city populations to move to the suburbs. This in turn encourages the destruction of forests, farm lands and wetlands.

One of the controversial issues in the United States is the lack of control over our borders. Many groups have taken up this cause. Two of the more vocal are *Zero Population Growth* and *Population Environment Balance*, both based in Washington D.C. Their philosophy is that although regions of the U.S. have wide open space it is not possible to locate people there because the carrying capacity of the land has already been reached and in most cases exceeded. The best way to get the land-people ratio stabilized is to limit immigration. Some other groups point to this seemingly idle land and encourage more immigration but when immigrants are permitted to enter the country most of them settle in the urban areas of California, Florida, New York and Texas, our most populous states.

Another area of concern is our involvement in the population of foreign countries. Many people, including some influential legislators, believe that when we send help in the form of medicines and food to needy countries we help to increase their populations and these countries seem to have no sense of responsibility.

Years ago, an editorial in *Bioscience, Feb. 1969* stated this philosophy when it said We give "food to the malnourished populations of the world that cannot or will not take very substantial measures to control their own reproductive rates" and this is "inhuman, immoral and irresponsible."

Regardless of your feelings about the subject, in the time it took to read this chapter, the population of the world increased by 5,200 people.

UNITED STATES: MOST POPULATED METROPOLITAN AREAS(in millions 1995)

New York	14.6	Detroit	3.0
Los Angeles	10.1	Dallas	2.8
Chicago	6.5	Washington	2.6
Philadelphia	4.0	Boston	2.5
San Francisco	4.0	Houston	2.3
Miami	3.5		

UNITED STATES: MOST POPULATED STATES (in millions,1995)

California	31.3	Illinois	11.7
Texas	18.3	Ohio	11.1
New York	18.2	Michigan	9.5
Florida	13.7	New Jersey	7.9
Pennsylvania	12.1	North Carolina	7.0

UNITED STATES: LEAST POPULATED STATES (in millions,1995)

Wyoming	0.5	South Dakota	0.7
Vermont	0.6	Montana	0.9
Alaska	0.6	Rhode Island	1.0
North Dakota	0.6	Idaho	1.1
Delaware	0.7	New Hampshire	1.1

7 FOREST RESOURCES

We have only to look about us to see that we live in a world of wood. The people of the United States use more wood per capita than any other nation. Wood provides us with over ten thousand different products. Indeed, it can be argued that humans are products of the forest.

THE VALUE OF FORESTS

Forests provide us with:

1. **Fuel** - More people in the world use wood for fuel than any other energy source. As the fossil fuel reserves decrease there will be a greater demand for wood as fuel. Unfortunately, some areas such as Haiti and sub-Sahara Africa have been completely denuded of forests and people living there have to rely on grass, dried manure and brush to cook their one meal a day. In places such as India, the use of dried manure for fuel deprives the soil of much needed fertilizer. This conflict of use damages the soil and further adds to the poverty of that area.

2. **Wildlife Habitat** - Forests contain more wildlife per acre than any other ecosystem. Forests bordering the Tundra are refuge areas for caribou. The Tropical Rainforest contains more than half the species of vegetation and animals found on earth. Unfortunately the rainforest is being cut over at the rate of 60 acres a minute to make room for cattle ranching and cropland.

3. **Flood Control** - There is virtually no runoff of water from a healthy forest area. This cuts down on soil erosion as well as flooding. Denuded, gullied and overgrazed areas can be rehabilitated by planting trees.

4. **Building and other Materials**
Almost every house in the United States contains wood as the main structural component. It does not seem likely that any other material will soon be used to replace wood in house construction. Forest products also include paper, rayon and cellulose.

5. **Recreation** - Our national and state forests provide a wealth of recreation. The Forest Service under the U.S. Department of Agriculture manages 156 forest districts. These amount to over 191 million acres of trees. The national forests provide great areas for camping, fishing, hunting, hiking and photography.

6. **Scientific Information** - Thousands of scientific studies are conducted annually in our forest systems. These encompass such areas as entomology, natural history, game management, ornithology, ecology as well as forestry. Methods of improving forests and forest management are always being sought.

MAJOR FOREST REGIONS OF THE
UNITED STATES

If the land is left untended in a wet climate the eventual result is a climax forest. For instance, if a farmer in New York State abandoned his fields and no one bothered them for ninety years and the farmer returned he would find a forest dominated by beech, maple and hemlock. This is the climax forest of that region.

The evolution of a bare field into forest progresses from (a) grass and low plants to (b) shrubs to (c) saplings to (d) forests of sun-loving species, to (e) forest of shade tolerant species. In each of these successive stages there are animals which prefer them for habitat. Each stage has its own plant and animal species.

In the United States our basic climax forest regions are:

(1) **Northern Evergreens** - This area stretches from Minnesota east to Maine and from southeastern Canada south to central Pennsylvania and along the Great Lakes. It is marked by beech, maple and hemlock in the

7-1 Forests provide us with more than 5,000 different products. The living forest produces oxygen, regulates temperatures, is a home to wildlife and provides us with recreation.

southern portion and white and red pine in the north as well as spruce and fir further north.

(2) **Central Hardwoods** - The hardwoods, mainly of oak and maple, inhabit the area south of the northern evergreens and continue to the northern portions of Louisiana, Mississippi, Alabama and Georgia. This is the home of our hardwood products industry. Furniture is manufactured in Asheville North Carolina and hardwood flooring in central Tennessee.

(3) **Southern Pine** - This is the coniferous region of the Deep South and the home of longleaf and loblolly pine. It forms in the north along the coasts of North Carolina and covers most of Louisiana, Mississippi, Alabama and Georgia as well as northern Florida. This was the traditional home of naval stores when sailing ships looked for sources of tar and turpentine. Pine is still a major wood for the home building trades.

(4) **Northwest Fir** - The Pacific Northwest with its huge temperate rainforest has been the scene of much controversy between environmentalists and loggers. The logging industry had become accustomed to getting access to public lands at unbelievably low prices. They were cutting off the old growth forests with little thought to the future when environmentalists used the Endangered Species Act to inhibit their voracious appetites for inexpensive lumber. The large spruce and Douglas Fir trees have been momentarily saved for future generations. The Northwest Fir region encompasses western Washington and Oregon. Some Douglas fir trees are more than a thousand years old and over 200 feet high. They rival the giant redwoods which grow to their south.

(5) **Mixed Evergreens** - South of the northwest fir and spruce grow the giant redwoods of southern Oregon and northern California. California is also home to the sugar and ponderosa pine, both valuable species of trees for the lumber industry.

(6) **Rocky Mountain** - These are large

7-2 In the past, the U.S. Forest Service has sold trees ,such as this ,for less than one dollar.

patches of forest isolated along the slopes of the Rocky Mountains just below the snow and alpine meadows. Ponderosa, white and sugar pine are dominant here. Unfortunately, cattle and sheep are allowed to graze on much of these lands and regeneration of the forests is a problem.

HARVESTING THE FORESTS

The first European settlers to come to America viewed the forests as something to be overcome and conquered. They never gave much thought to conservation and sustained yield. Today we realize that we are very dependent upon forests and forest products and need to preserve forests not only for our own uses but for those of future generations.

The first Federal Forest Reserves Act of 1891 set aside timber reserves in the Yellowstone area. The act authorized the president to set aside more federal lands to ensure future timber supplies and protect water resources.

The Multiple Use and Sustained Yield Act of 1960 was an attempt to put the U.S. Forest Service in a position to govern the forests without undue influence of the logging industry. The multiple use of forests for flood control, erosion control, preservation and recreation took a back seat to logging. During the 1960s, 70s and 80s the Forest Service permitted unprecedented logging. Not only were trees sold to loggers at ridiculously low prices but the forest service lost money by building roads into wilderness areas for the benefit of loggers. The only national forest to show a profit during those times was the Allegheny National Forest in Pennsylvania. The rest lost millions of dollars.

There are three basic methods of cutting forests - clear cutting, strip cutting and selective cutting. The type of harvest depends on many factors including financial profit as well as conservation.

Clear cutting is the standard logging practice in Maine and the Pacific Northwest. An area is cut of all timber and brush and the cutover area can be left to regenerate trees by wind blowing seeds from those border trees left standing. In some instances seeding is done by helicopter or by hand scattering. However, most forests are replanted by hand with two year old seedlings.

A clear cut area is not pleasant to see but it is an effective harvesting method. If clear cutting is done on a rotation basis then a sustained yield can be maintained. This method also permits quick harvesting of a large number of trees and for a specific purpose. Clear cutting encourages the growth of shade intolerant trees such as pine, walnut,

fir and aspen.

Clear cutting accelerates water runoff and therefore encourages flooding. With an increase in water runoff there is an increase in soil erosion. Trees on the edges of clear cuts are more likely to be blown over by winds since they no longer have the protection of surrounding trees. It also limits the carrying capacity of wildlife. And, the brush and slash accompanying clear cutting is always a fire hazard.

However, clear cutting is the only method of accelerating the growth of shade intolerant species of trees. Once brush starts to grow it becomes home to deer, rabbits, grouse, elk, moose and many songbirds. Clear cutting can also be used to remove a small portion of a forest infected with diseases or pests.

Strip cutting is a variation of clear cutting. Strip cutting involves only cutting a path of about a hundred yards through the forest and leaving stands of about a hundred yards on each side. This gives the benefit of growing shade intolerant trees and fire breaks in the cut over strips. This also minimizes the loss of water and soil during heavy rains.

Selective cutting is a search and cut method of harvesting. Loggers go into a forest and search out the tree species they desire. Under these conditions trees may be harvested and a forest of uneven age is maintained. This preserves the forest ecosystem where the clear cut method does not. This system, although more expensive than clear cutting, results in a high rate of natural reseeding.

One big disadvantage of selective cutting is that the best types of timber are harvested and the less desirable types are left behind. Unless the forest is properly managed this could be a serious problem. Another disadvantage of selective cutting is that it is not useful for regenerating shade intolerant species such as pine and fir which are in big demand for lumber and plywood.

7-3 Logs floating down the Columbia River in the Pacific Northwest. These logs were cut from federal lands.

Selective cutting can be made on a rotation basis and a sustained yield can be accomplished. It also reduces the fire hazard to forests because there is little slash left behind. Selective cutting also inhibits monoculture.

MONOCULTURE

The U.S. Department of Agriculture has encouraged farmers and large land owners to begin tree farms. These usually result in monoculture or the growing of one species of tree. The advantage to monoculture is that a particular species of tree can be grown for a specific purpose such as pulpwood or furniture veneer.

Monoculture is an efficient method of producing large volumes of timber. Since the trees are all the same age they can be harvested with a minimum of expense. It also is less expensive in the use of fertilizers and pesticides than mixed cultures. And, it makes the growing of shade intolerant species possible.

Monoculture does not encourage a forest ecosystem to develop. Once the ecosystem becomes established it is cut over and a new rotation begun. There is no development of litter on the forest floor. Monoculture fosters the overuse of fertilizers and pesticides as a solution to many growth problems.

Monoculture is more susceptible to diseases and pests. An insect infestation is a tragedy since it is easy to move from one tree to another in the monoculture tree stand whereas a gypsy moth which prefers oak trees might have a hard time finding the next one in a mixed forest.

FOREST PROBLEMS

The major forest problems include insects, fungi, fires, flooding, grazing animals, storms and overcutting. As conservationists we can do something about all of these problems except storms.

Among the insects that have been especially destructive to American forests in the past are gypsy moths, bark beetles, budworms, sawflies, bagworms, tent caterpillars and weevils. The gypsy moths prefer oaks. They have slowly made their way westward from New England where they escaped from an experiment to produce silk. Bark beetles eat the cambium layer of the bark and girdle trees. They have also been responsible for the spread of various fungi such as that which causes the Dutch Elm Disease.

Budworms kill the terminal buds of trees as well as defoliating them. Bagworms strip spruce trees of their needles and weevils kill the sprouting leaders of pine and spruce trees causing them to grow crooked.

Tent caterpillars build huge unsightly webs in trees such as wild black cherry. Their larva move out from the protective nests and devour the leaves. They return to the nests for protection and to pupate and produce the moths which in turn lay more eggs.

Probably the most destructive of the forest pests are the fungi. These produce such diseases as rusts, wilts and blights. Particularly bad in pine forests are the white pine wilt, brown spot, western red rot and root rot. Oak forests are plagued with oak wilt. Elm trees get the Dutch Elm Disease.

Insects are controlled by spraying insecticides, burning infested areas and in some cases hand removal. Fungi are controlled by spraying, pruning, burning, placing mechanical barriers and premature harvesting of trees. There is also some progress in pH soil research and the incidence of fungi infections. Research also indicates that planting certain species of trees in close proximity encourages certain types of fungi.

FIRE AND THE FOREST

About three hundred fires break out in the American forests every day. Most of these are quickly brought under control. About ten percent of the fires are caused by lightning and ninety percent by humans. Most of the human caused fires are not accidental. Often they are set by firebugs, people who get a thrill out of seeing fires. Many are also set by people seeking revenge for real or imagined slights by the forest owners.

A controlled burn is fire set purposely by foresters. These have low flames and are constantly monitored as they spread along the forest floor. The purpose of these controlled burns are usually to get rid of underbrush which may cause a more serious fire later.

They are also used to eliminate competition of plants with trees. This technique is used extensively in the Southern Pine region to prepare the soil as a seedbed for the next generation of trees. It also stimulates the activity of soil bacteria which is essential for good tree growth.

The National Park Service has a policy to let a natural fire burn itself out even if it means the loss of trees. The philosophy here relies on the fact that nature has created fires over the centuries in order to establish an ecosystem relying on burnt over woodlands. This policy was temporarily abandoned in the great Yellowstone Park fire of 1988 when fires threatened human habitation.

Forest fires are of three types - soil fires, ground fires and crown fires. Soil fires smolder at root level. These may burn for years before they can be controlled. It relies on heavy dry humus, moss and other almost peat conditions.

The ground fires stick to the underbrush and are low but extensive burns. Even though ground fires are considered beneficial to commercial monoculture forests they can be detrimental to a mixed forest ecosystem.

The crown fires are the most destructive as the flames leap form tree top to tree top. Deer and other creatures of the forest run for their lives. With a good wind these fires take months to get under control. Their damage runs in the millions of dollars. Besides the Yellowstone Fire, in 1988, over 18,000 acres of forest burned in Colorado, another 17,000 burned in South Dakota and 15,000 acres in Alaska.

Forests can be protected to some extent by cutting wide swaths through them to serve as fire lanes. Unless there is an exceptionally strong wind the fire is stopped at the lane.

The Forest Service uses spotters on high towers to watch for fires. When an obvious fire is identified the spotters call in the azimuth to a central location. By plotting the

7-4 Clear cutting of public lands in Oregon. The road in the photo was built by the Forest Service to facilitate the removal of logs.

various azimuths on a map the headquarters can identify the exact location of the fire.

Once the fire is located a photography team is dispatched to the spot in helicopters and video tapes are made of the blaze. This might appear to be wasting time but the nature of the fire determines what kind of equipment is necessary to fight it. If the fire is severe then smoke jumpers are sent in to start controlling it with techniques such as back burning. This is burning material back into the fire and when the two flames meet the fire cannot progress any further. Helicopters are also used to dump water and flame retardent chemicals on the fire.

CONSERVATION OF THE FOREST

The best conservation method for preserving the forest is not to cut it. However, that is not feasible. So we have to make adjustments in our forest practices and use of wood products. We can use wood substitutes such as abundant aluminum for scarce hard furniture woods. Aluminum and steel can be used in house construction.

We can recycle paper products to save trees as well as landfill space. Presently about a third of all landfill material is paper.

There is a need to upgrade the eastern forests of the United States. Much of the eastern forest is in the hands of private owners and most eastern states have agriculture departments which work in close harmony with woodlot owners. They offer seminars in woodlot management and disease and pest control.

The United States can preserve its forests by cutting down on exports and increasing imports. Countries such as Canada, Sweden, Norway and Finland have small populations and extensive forests which they are willing to export at prices lower than those of the United States.

One of the big world problems is the destruction of the tropical rainforest. This "green lung" of the earth is being cut at the rate of 90 acres a minute. The rainforest has more than fifty percent of all plant and animal species left on earth. The rainforest is being cut mostly to furnish specialty woods for the furniture industry and to clear land to raise hamburger cattle which is exported to the fast food restaurants of the United States and Europe.

If we lose the rainforest gene pool we will have lost one of the great riches of the earth. More than ninety percent of all prescription drugs have been developed or created from plants and most of them have been from rainforest plants. We don't know how many more life saving drugs can be developed from rainforest plants but we do know there are unlimited possibilities there.

CONTROVERSY IN NATIONAL FOREST POLICY

Each year, enough timber is cut on America's national forests to build about one million houses, nearly twenty percent of the nation's timber harvest. Millions of head of livestock graze on the forest floor. Half of the nation's big game animals and coldwater fish live there.

Environmentalists, ranchers, motorcyclists and timber companies are engaged in a fierce and emotion debate of the future of the forests. At the center is the U.S. Forest Service, the federal agency that will determine the future of the forests and the resources they contain.

The Forest Service is the largest and oldest of the public land agencies. The agency's holdings constitute a land empire larger than many countries of the world. There are 156 National Forest encompassing 191 million acres. This is equal to the total area of Illinois, Iowa, Michigan, Wisconsin and Minnesota.

Controversy erupted in the 1970s when the environmental movement challenged the growing demand by timber companies to cut more trees on public lands. This controversy became intense in the Pacific Northwest, in the "old-growth" forests. This area contains ancient Douglas fir and hemlock stands, some trees more than a thousand years old.

In assessing the controversy, Jay D. Hair, president of the National Wildlife Federation (NWF) said "Old growth is attractive to timber companies because it represents profits. The trees are large, they produce high quality timber and they are relatively accessible. In short, the economics of cutting old growth are highly favorable".

Almost all of the old growth on private land in Washington, Oregon and northern California has been cut. What remains is on public land, primarily in the national forests. If cutting at former rates continues in these forests they will be gone in twenty years.

Unfortunately the Forest Service has been selling off trees to timber interests at huge losses each year. The Forest Service losses amounted to an average $343 million a year over eleven years starting in 1983. Taxpayers subsidized these losses.

It takes about one hundred years for a Lodgepole Pine to reach 65 feet. Under present regulations a timber company can buy the right to take this tree for a dollar. Also, consider the fact that the U.S. Government also builds free roads to give loggers access to these trees. In 1995, the Forest Service planned to have 580,000 miles of roads through our National Forests, more than enough to reach to the moon and back. The interstate highway system in 1995 was 40,000 miles.

The Forest Service is bound by law to manage the forests for all their values - this includes preserving wildlife, protecting watersheds and providing recreation. Timber harvesting is just one aspect of the obligations of forest management, yet it dominates federal expenditures in the national forests. Many organizations such as the Sierra Club, National Wildlife Federation and the Wilderness Society monitor the situation in the national forests. However, they do not have the financial resources to match those of the big timber companies and unfortunately our political system is heavily influenced by contributions to political campaigns. This does not bode well for our national forests, one of our greatest natural resources.

Land Owned by U.S. Government
% of total land in selected states

Nevada	82.3	Oregon	48.2
Alaska	67.8	Arizona	43.3
Utah	63.8	Colorado	34.1
Idaho	62.6	New Mexico	33.1
California	60.9	Washington	29.0
Wyoming	48.8	Montana	27.7

7-5 Fire fighters battle a small blaze. Cutting and stacking trees in a row helps the fire to die out before it gets too big.

8 RANGELAND RESOURCES

Rangelands were the grazing grounds for wild animals long before there were people. These are areas of low vegetation sometimes called grasslands although grass is only one component of them. Besides grasses, the rangelands have reeds and rushes, forbs and brush. Forbs are low succulent green plants such as the dandelion. Reeds and rushes are usually found near wet spots and these have round stems.

People raise about ten billion animals on rangelands. Most of these are ruminants, animals that have cloven hooves and chew cud. Most of these are cattle, sheep and goats.

There are many different classifications of rangelands in the world. The large areas are designated as steppes, tundra and savanna. There are sub-classifications within these large ecosystems.

When European settlers first came to North America they crossed the Mississippi River and headed west. Here they found wide open spaces. Here were bison grazing in unbelievable numbers. The principle grasses at that time were Big Bluestem, Bluegrass and Buffalo Grass. Other grasses of importance to the bison were Green Needlegrass, Canada Wild Rye and Sideoats Grama. These grasses along with the forbs supported millions of animals and the native people that depended upon them for their livelihood.

In a very short period of time, from roughly 1840 to 1890 the bison were diminished to a few hundred animals. Reports state that the last bison in the wild was killed in 1894.

This was only the first of many animals that were to be depleted by the European pioneers. However, the story of the bison has a happy note. From the roughly 200 animals found in wayside zoos and a few kept by settlers as curiosities the federal government along with some concerned citizens were able to bring the bison herd back to over 200,000 million animals in the next fifty years.

When World War I was in full swing around 1917 there was a move on to raise more beef cattle and western lands under federal control were opened to full scale ranching. After the war, ranching continued and the western rangelands deteriorated since the people who used them did not take care of them and the federal government was lax in its administration of these lands.

Soon, western lands were put to the plow and the disastrous droughts of the 1930s created the famous "dust bowl" which literally blew the land away.

Conservationists were able to persuade Congress to pass the Taylor Grazing Control Act in 1934 which only affected federal lands. It didn't help much but at least the federal government was getting more involved in preserving one of our great national treasures.

The western rangelands continued to deteriorate until the creation of the Bureau of Land Managment (BLM) in 1959. This organization was placed under the Department of Interior and was given the assignment of rehabilitating the rangelands. In their first inventory of lands only eighteen percent was found to be in good shape.

The BLM started a program of planting windbreaks or shelterbelts where trees were planted to cut down on wind erosion and evaporation. They also started a program of deferred grazing and allotment of cattle and sheep on ranges. A program of reseeding the desirable grasses mentioned earlier was also begun.

Unfortunately, the BLM assumed its mandate was to create good rangeland for grazing cattle and sheep and it worked

8-1 Bunch grass in Idaho classified as "poor" rangeland. It takes twenty-five acres of this land to support one steer. Plowing this land would open it up to wind erosion.

toward that end. Its other mandates of preservation, conservation and recreation were pretty much ignored. The land continued to be abused and only with the election of President Bill Clinton and his appointment of Bruce Babbit as Secretary of Interior did the influence of cattle barons on Congress begin to decline.

RANGE MANAGEMENT TECHNIQUES

Management of rangelands begins with an inventory of its vegetation. Plants are classified as decreasers, increasers or invaders. Decreasers are the desirable plants such as Big Bluestem that decrease when the land begins to become overgrazed. Increasers are the less desirable plants which begin to increase with overgrazing. These include Kentucky Bluegrass which is not as desirable in the western variety. The invaders are very undesirable species such as yarrow, cactus, ragweed and thistle.

Range managers also note the amount of mulch on the ground. This is the dead plant material that covers the ground under vegetation. This has implications for the future organic content of the soil.

The condition of soil is also noted. A thick spongy layer of erosion resistant sod is excellent. Sometimes the pH of the soil is taken in order to determine specific needs. However, most rangeland managers can look at the vegetation and tell whether it needs fertilizing or liming. Plants such as sorrel indicate a highly acid soil.

Once the condition of the range is ascertained the carrying capacity of each section can be determined. This is the ability of a particular section to graze a certain number of animals without extensive deterioration. The carrying capacity is diminished when there are wild species competing with domestic species for the range. Presently, the competing wild species include jack rabbits, elk, deer, antelope, mice, prairie dogs, rats and even grasshoppers and crickets.

Grass turns solar energy into chlorophyll and green plants. The grazing animals get their energy by eating the plants and we get our energy by eating the grazing animals. Therefore, we are a product of solar energy.

The tips of grass can be eaten without affecting its growth since the plant grows from the roots and sends up a continuous stream of blades of grass. The grass can be continually grazed as long as the grazing

8-2 A cattle round-up in Montana. More than half the world's arable land is used to raise livestock. Livestock consumes 40 percent of the world's grain.

animals do not get too close to the sod. When they begin to eat into the sod (overgraze) they destroy the metabolic reserve of the plant. This part of the plant is necessary for plant survival since it is where the plant sends energy down to preserve and enhance the roots. Grasses may have root systems extending down to six feet and much of the plants energy is stored in them. This enables the plant to survive long periods of drought and brief periods of overgrazing. By eating the metabolic reserve the grazing animal kills the plant.

In order to keep cattle in a certain section of range the managers or the cattlemen control the water and salt supply. If there is a stream in the section then it is difficult to get cattle to move to another section. But cattle need salt and by moving salt blocks to the new section cattle will eventually follow.

If the range is overrun with undesirable plants such as mesquite the area may be sprayed with a herbicide which will kill all shrubs. Once the shrubs are killed and left to dry they can be burned. This can also be done with prickly pear cactus, another plant pest of our western rangelands.

After burning, the land can be seeded with the desired grasses. Seeding used to be by hand and broadcasting. This resulted in a high seed loss to birds and mice. The exposed seeds were often killed by cold winter. Today, seeding is completed with drill machinery which punches seeds into the ground.

In African countries grasshoppers (or locusts as they are called) get about one third of the grain crop. They also get a good portion of our western range plants. Grasshoppers multiply best in poor rangelands and if the rangeland is healthy the number of grasshoppers is severely diminished. It is better to have this natural control of insects than to blanket the land with insecticides.

Sometimes there are more jack rabbits in numbers than there are cattle on the range. A large number of jack rabbits encourages increaser and invader plants. So again, maintaining a healthy range controls these pests.

Cattle and sheep are also affected by the same predators that cut into the wild antelope and rabbit populations. These include coyotes, wolves, mountain lions, bobcats and even bear. The worst of these is the coyote. Today, around ninety thousand coyotes are destroyed annually on our federal western rangelands. Unfortunately, the ranchers want a widespread destruction of coyotes but reason tells us that the coyote hunts should be held only in those regions where coyotes are a nuisance and actually killing lambs. Coyotes, of course, do not attack cattle. In fact, putting cattle in with the sheep guarantees that coyotes will leave the sheep alone. Coyotes keep mice, rats and jack rabbits from overpopulation. They do more good than harm. By destroying the grass eaters, the coyote expands the range for domestic animals. The value of the added range outweighs the value of the few lambs that are taken by coyotes each year.

MAJOR PROBLEMS WITH RANGELANDS

Our southwestern rangelands have become endangered. What was once healthy ranges in southern California, Nevada, Arizona, New Mexico and Texas have become deserts. Overgrazing coupled with drought have caused the land to enter into a process of desertification. This is the conversion of rangeland to desert conditions. It is extremely bad in Africa where the Sahara Desert is advancing at the rate of ten miles per year. Some progress has been made in Africa in abating this advance.

Desertification can also occur when rangeland has been irrigated over a period of years. A build-up of mineral salts forms on the surface. This necessitates plowing deeper and deeper to mix the salts with soil and eventually ends up with a sterile soil. This salinization of soil can also occur when salt lakes or ocean water infiltrates the ground water system under the rangeland.

The best solution to desertification and salinization is to take the rangeland out of production. However, this is difficult to do in places such as Africa where starvation is everybody's neighbor.

One of the solutions to rangeland deterioration might be to increase the use of native wild animals on the ranges instead of the usual cattle and sheep. Some experiments with bison, yaks, antelopes, wildebeeste, llamas and water buffalo have been successful. Reindeer and musk ox "ranching" have been successful in the cold lands of the tundra.

Rangelands make up fifty six percent of the land of North America. The cattle and sheep industry annually accounts for just under ten percent of our Gross National Product. It is important that we conserve and make wise use of this valuable resource.

We should be concerned about rangelands in other sections of the world since loss of potential food producing soils will affect everyone. Almost half the earth's populated surface is rangeland and almost half of this is used to graze livestock. The other half is too dry or too cold for conventional ranching.

Many countries with grazing lands are too poor to curb their use. In more affluent countries such as Canada, United States, Argentina and Australia we can afford the luxury of delayed grazing and other conservation schemes.

Good rangeland management involves limiting the number of animals on a range to coincide with its carrying capacity and excluding livestock from sensitive riparian areas. In the United States there is a need for

8-3 Grazed and ungrazed rangeland in the American West.

a complete revision of the use of federally owned rangelands. Perhaps, we should eliminate subsidized ranching on our public lands and let the livestock industry meet free market competition.

WATERSHEDS ON RANGELANDS

Riparian zones are strips and patches of vegetation that surround streams and wet places. Riparian zones act as green ribbons of life that bind the landscape into one ecosystem. If you change the riparian zone, you change the ecosystem.

Riparian zones make up about five percent of our rangelands but they often govern the activities on the other 95 percent. For instance, in Oregon, livestock get 81 percent of their forage from riparian zones which make up only two percent of the area.

Riparian zone ecosystems contain groups of plants, animals, soil and water that comprise the biotic communities. These zones are found not only along streams but around seeps, springs and lakes. In arid regions, they are often the only place that is green.

Riparian areas provide food and shelter for rodents and small birds that hawks, eagles and owls hunt for food. Riparian zones store water, filter it, trap sediment and reduce floods. The zones act as pipelines that carry clean water downstream for use in cities and irrigation of crops.

Riparian areas which are critical to a healthy ecosystem attract livestock. If not properly managed, livestock can damage riparian vegetation beyond its ability to recover and destroy stream-bank structures.

Livestock grazing in riparian areas often results in higher stream temperatures, excessive sediment in the stream channel, high coliform bacteria, stream channel widening which reduces water depth, change or elimination of vegetation, lowering of the water table and gradual stream channel trenching or braiding.

62

8-4 Each year more than ninety thousand coyotes are killed by the U. S. Department of Agriculture as a service to ranchers. Most ranchers are under the impression that coyotes are detrimental to livestock. Coyotes eat jack rabbits, kangaroo rats and mice which feed on grasses. The added range the coyotes preserve more than compensates for the taking of a few lambs.

Beaver, waterfowl and moose may disappear from an entire drainage area once riparian shrubs die. When habitat for rodents and small birds disappears, predators leave or hunt other prey.

In most federal rangeland riparian areas, managers already know ways to reduce or eliminate livestock and other impacts, such as road construction, logging or off-road vehicles. This knowledge can't be evenly applied until range managers have time to work with livestock owners and other public interests to develop or revise grazing management plans.

Improving riparian management often requires managing livestock in radically new ways. Changing from mid-summer to late winter or fall grazing may be the solution. Or in some cases, spring grazing of riparian areas and the removal of cattle before the hot dry part of summer will allow riparian vegetation to thrive. Unless people who own and manage the livestock are committed to the changes needed for riparian protection and improvement, the changes and improvements will come slowly.

THE BUREAU OF LAND MANAGEMENT

The Bureau of Land Managment (BLM) administers what remains of the nation's once vast land holdings, the public domain. This once stretched from the Appalachian Mountains to the Pacific Ocean. Of the 1.8 billion acres of public land originally acquired by the United States, two-thirds went to individuals, industries and the states. Of that remaining, much was set aside for national forests, wildlife refuges, national parks and monuments and other public purposes. This left BLM to manage about 272 million acres, about one-eighth of the national land surface.

The BLM also manages the mineral estate under 572 million acres, 300 million acres of which are administered or owned by other agencies or private interests. Most of the lands are located in eleven western states, including Alaska, although small parcels are scattered across the eastern United States.

Multiple Use Mandate

Recreation: BLM manages a full range of recreation activities including the Wild and Scenic River System, National Trails and four million acres of lakes and reservoirs used for fishing and other water activities.

Forestry: There are over 90 million acres of forested land managed by the BLM. Most of this is in Alaska but with at least 26 million acres in the lower 48 states.

Wilderness: BLM manages 25 wilderness areas in eight states. There are also about 900 wilderness study areas covering more than 25 million acres under BLM supervision.

Range: BLM manages livestock grazing on 1,265 million acres of public lands. In 1995, almost 19,000 ranchers grazed livestock on public lands. About 90 percent of these ranchers had less than 500 head operations.

Cultural Resources: There are over 150,000 identifiable cultural resources on public lands. There are 350 archaeological and historic properties entered in the National Register of Historic Places and an additional 1,200 considered to have significant values. These range from campsites of the hemisphere's earliest human inhabitants to physical reminders of the historic setting of the West.

Wildlife: BLM manages wildlife habitat for more than 3,000 species, including 140 threatened or endangered plant and animal species. It manages habitat for one out of every five big game animals in the United States, including caribou, brown and grizzly bears, desert bighorn sheep, moose, mule deer and antelope.

Wild Horses and Burros: There are more than 43,000 wild horses and burros on public lands. Any citizen with good intent can apply to the BLM for a free horse or burro. The citizen must pay for immunization shots and transportation.

Lands: The BLM issues leases, rights-of-way and use permits for a wide variety of uses of public lands and parks. This includes such things as power line transmission , petroleum product collection, motion picture filming and recreational events.

One of the controversial aspects of BLM management is the legal issuing of mineral rights to developers. The original laws passed in 1875 are still in effect. This allows developers of oil, gas, geothermal, coal, radioactive materials, building materials and metal ores to obtain the right to exploit these for two dollars and seventy five cents an acre. Most of these leases are worth millions of dollars and the system is simply taxpayers subsidizing industries which could well afford to pay the current value for these leases.

Public lands provide about fifty percent of the nation's potash, forty-five percent of its sodium compounds and seventy percent of its lead. Public lands in the West are supporting a new gold rush. Fourteen of the top twenty five producing U.S. gold mines are on public lands. The rights to these were purchased at unbelievably low prices.

Federally owned rangelands account for 55% of the total rangelands in the United States. These lands are no longer wild and must be managed with an eye to preservation and future use. Can we continue to manage these once wild lands for domestic livestock and eliminate the native animals which once roamed freely on them? Are we now the caretakers of all land and animals and do we have an obligation to those animals we have displaced.

9 WILDLIFE RESOURCES

Human life and human experiences have evolved with wild plants and animals. We owe our very existence to these wild resources. In our distant past and in our present we have taken these wild plants and animals and domesticated them. That is, we have taken them from their wild habitat and created habitats for them in order for them to be more accessible to us.

Generally when we use the term wildlife, we are referring to the animal world. However, we must always bear in mind that we cannot separate the wild animals from the wild plants which are necessary for their survival, and ultimately for our own survival.

Wildlife resources affords humans many benefits. These resources can be classified as (1) economic (2) scientific (3) aesthetic, and (4) recreational. Each has its own value in making life richer and more comfortable for us.

Our economy is spurred on by the benefits from anglers, hunters, campers and bird watchers to mention only a few of the groups. These people spend millions of dollars pursuing their hobbies which enhances the general economy.

For instance there are over seventeen million hunters in the United States who buy licenses each year. The states of Texas and Pennsylvania each sell over a million hunting licenses annually. Pennsylvania's economy benefits directly from the purchase of these licenses and other fees to the tune of 500 million dollars annually. These hunters also spend money in motels, hunting lodges and restaurants each hunting season. They spend millions of dollars on guns and ammunition and hunting clothes. In the United States the hunting dog industry nets over ten million dollars each year.

The recreational uses of our wildlife and habitats include camping, hiking, trail bike riding, snowmobiling and bird watching.

Birders spend over a hundred million dollars a year just visiting birding "hot spots."

The scientific study of animals has given us many insights into our own behavior and illnesses. Practically every break-through in modern medicine has been by experimentation with animals. By studying bird migration and animal hibernation we know now that many people get depressed in winter due to the lack of sunlight.

In many parts of the world wildlife is a necessary supply of food. Even in American society we consume over ten million grouse, nine million deer, twenty million wild rabbits and two million hare each year. All of these harvested from the wild.

EXTINCTION

The fossil record indicates that millions of animals which once made earth their home are now extinct. They and their genes have disappeared from earth. We need not look at the fossil record to see that extinction is a fact of life , we only need look to our own recorded history. Birds such as the heath hen, passenger pigeon and great auk have all become extinct during the lifetime of the human species.

We like to blame such events as extinction on a particular circumstance but extinction is a combination of factors. Some of these factors are listed below.

Low Biotic Potential: Each species has a theoretical maximum of population growth if the resources available to them are unlimited and they are not hampered by such things as disease, predators and competition. If two flies mated in early March and their offspring and the offspring's offspring survived to mature then by the end of November the land portion of the world would be covered with flies to a depth of five feet.

This is a theoretical situation but we have many examples of real life events that have occurred in the past. A famous study of mule deer in the Kaibab National Forest of the Grand Canyon illustrates this point well. In 1906 the State of Arizona placed a bounty on the wolf, coyote and cougar. The National Forest is inside the boundaries of Arizona. Within fifteen years the predator population had been reduced to only a few hundred animals and the wolf population was wiped out completely. In the next twenty years the deer population which started out at about five thousand animals had soared to over a hundred thousand. This was well beyond the carrying capacity of the habitat. The deer ate just about everything they could reach and in the next six years the population began to crash with an annual starvation rate of sixteen thousand deer. The forest was severely damaged since a browse line emerged and no new seedlings were permitted to germinate since the deer ate these as fast as they came up. Seventy five years later this forest has still not recovered.

Competition and Survival: There are three stages of animal populations (1) production (2) competition, and (3) survival. Each animal species is capable of producing more offspring than the habitat will support. For instance, a pair of adult oysters will produce almost two million eggs. When those two million eggs hatch the young are subjected to intense competition for food. They must fight each other for food and they must fight other species such as clams, crayfish, squid and fish for the same food. Those oysters are also food for other species. Of those two million original oysters only two will survive to maturity. Those that survive will pass their survival genes on to the next generation. As a result, we continue to get oysters better adapted to the environment. Keep in mind that you are here because your ancestors knew how to survive. They overcame tremendous obstacles in order to reproduce and have you as a final product.

Food Preferences: We classify animals into several categories for easy identification.

Herbivores are those that eat only plants. Carnivores eat only meat and omnivores eat both plants and meat. The range of carnivores is larger than the range of herbivores. Carnivores are predators or scavengers and when the population of herbivores decreases so does the population of carnivores.

Some animals have such specialized diets that they are in danger of extinction. The panda eats only a few species of bamboo shoots, the koala bear eats only eucalyptus leaves and when these plants are threatened by disease or bad weather then the animals that feed on them are likewise threatened. The Everglade Kite, a large eagle-like bird, feeds only on one species of snail. If the snail should suddenly succumb to a disease or pollution then the Everglade Kite must change its eating habits or perish.

Predators and Parasites: Predators are animals that hunt and kill other animals (the prey). Parasites are animals that live on or off of other animals but do not necessarily kill the animal. Cougars, coyotes and wolves are predators. These eat such animals as birds, rabbits and browsers.

The parasites of the animal world are mostly worms such as tapeworms, lungworms, heartworms and various fly larva. There are also parasites which cause diseases. These are mostly protozoans and viruses.

Technically plants are preyed upon by browsing animals and they too have parasites which limit their populations. We must not forget that plants have similar DNA (stuff that makes up our genes and chromosomes) as animals. We are all interrelated in that we have the same basic biological molecules within us.

Life Cycles: Wildlife studies have given us some convenient methods of identifying the population patterns of animals. Most of these are based on carrying capacity, that is, the population of a species that a habitat can support on a sustainable basis.

A stable population may have its ups and downs from year to year but basically it remains at the same average number of individuals over period of years. These populations have a good balance of food, predators, competition and reproduction.

An irruptive population is one that rises sharply. This may occur when there is a series of favorable weather conditions which increases the food supply beyond that which keeps the population in balance. Once the irruption occurs the condition will continue for a number of years until the predator or lack of food in the ecosystem brings it back to normal. In the case of the mule deer of the Kaibab the destruction of predators was largely responsible for the irruption.

A cyclic population peaks and then crashes periodically. The cycle is predictable and is related to reproduction, predators, and since this usually occurs in herbivores to overgrazing. Most biology students are familiar with the lemmings of the far north. Their principal predators are the fox, owl and lynx. The lemmings have a population burst every three years. This is due to factors listed previously. As the lemmings increase, an increase in fox and owls is a year behind. Due to the increased food supply they increase their populations and so the northern owls and foxes peak about every three years, just after the lemmings.

· Other animals which have a cyclic population include the red-tailed hawk and the snowshoe hare. There is also a cycle which includes muskrats (prey) and mink (predator).

Habitat Destruction: As our population grows we must expand our activities to compensate for this growth. People need food, clothing and shelter as well as other necessities and non-necessities to make our life comfortable. As we engage in building cities, highways, cutting trees and farming we destroy habitat needed by wildlife. What seems to be left in America are islands of wildlife habitat, sometimes called ecological islands. These are small areas surrounded by human habitation and influence.

As these islands are further diminished by encroachment of humans they support less wildlife. Each species has its own critical population size. If the population falls below this critical level then it is too small for the species to survive. Also, these smaller island habitats encourage in-breeding which produces inferior offspring.

We have tried to preserve wildlife by creating a series of parks such as our National Parks and National Forests. However, these are not enough to keep many species from biotic impoverishment. Many studies have confirmed that the number of species in our national parks have been decreasing over the years. Many parks are simply too small to support major predator species such as the grizzly bear and wolves.

Only two national parks on North America have been able to support their original number of species. These are the Jasper-Banff series of parkland in western Canada and the Yellowstone complex of Wyoming. Glacier National Park has done well in protecting most of its species but the rest of the park system has lost over twenty five percent of their original numbers.

Hunting: Generally hunting is divided into commercial hunting and sport hunting. Commercial hunting provides food and other products for a large number of people. Commercial hunting has contributed to the extinction of the passenger pigeon and the great auk, a large bird that once lived along the North Atlantic Coast. Commercial hunting has been responsible for the near demise of the bison, rhinoceros, tiger and whales. Today, commercial hunting in Sierra Leone and other west central countries of Africa are killing off the monkey populations. These are used for food. Unless some

9-1 A wildlife specialist records the habitat of the Black Bear which needs at least 40 square miles of forest per pair to survive.

international agency interferes, the monkeys of that region would be eliminated in the next few years.

Sport hunting , on the other hand, has been responsible for the protection of many animal species. No animal that has ever been under the control of game commissions has ever become extinct. Through taxes, sport hunters have been responsible for the purchase of thousands of acres of wilderness which have been protected from urbanization and farming. These gamelands protect, not only game species, but hundreds of other non-game species as well. There are over 400 National Wildlife Refuges in the United States and these were purchased largely from the taxes and license fees of duck and waterfowl hunters.

Non-adaptive Behavior: Many species cannot adapt to changes in their environment. Deer, which has a range of about one square mile, refuse to move out of that territory even as it is being cut and destroyed. Moving deer to another location has proved to be unsuccessful. Only about four out of a hundred deer survive the move. The same is true for rabbits. Trapped rabbits which are

9-2 Student researchers gather fish stunned by electro-shocking. Data on the fish will be taken. The fish will be resusitated and released.

moved to a new habitat survive less than six months and the luckier ones survive up to a year.

PROTECTING OUR WILDLIFE HERITAGE

The Endangered Species Act was first passed in 1973. Since then, it has been modified several times. The act requires the U.S. Fish and Wildlife Service to identify species and classify them as endangered, threatened or not in danger. Endangered species are those that are in imminent danger of going extinct. In the United States (1995) this involved 36 mammals, 57 birds, 60 fish, 8 reptiles, 6 amphibians, 14 snails, 16 insects, 378 plants, 11 crustaceans and 50 clams. However, worldwide there are many more species threatened with extinction. Of these, there are 234 mammals and 141 birds.

A threatened species is one that is likely to become extinct if present practices involving

them continue. In the United States this involves 5 mammals, 15 reptiles, 8 birds, 32 fish, 4 amphibians, 7 snails, 6 clams, 2 crustaceans, 9 insects and 8 plants. The number worldwide is not high in this category but nevertheless those few species must be protected lest they move into the endangered category.

The Endangered Species Act also requires the U.S. Fish and Wildlife Service to identify the habitat of the endangered species and once identified, prevent destruction of that habitat. This part of the law was used successfully to stop the cutting of many old growth forests of the Pacific Northwest. The spotted owl received much publicity but the argument was not over owls but over cutting the old growth forests which is part of our American heritage.

The least costly method of saving plants and animals is by setting aside large tracts of land where a population of plants and animals can continue to survive without molestation by humans. Unless the habitat is extremely large, the animals and plants are afforded only temporary protection.

A costlier but effective approach to ecological preservation is the restoration of previously damaged lands. The industrialized world is busy making deals with rainforest countries to preserve this valuable asset. The rainforest has more than half the world's species of plants and animals. However, rainforests are located in poor countries and it is difficult to tell a farmer clearing the rainforest that he can't do that and we in the richer countries would prefer he returns to his village and live in poverty.

Since the rainforest countries are deep in debt there is some hope in the process of exchanging rainforest protection for the cancellation of debt. Many holders of the debt have agreed to do this and countries such as Brazil have participated in this debt exchange for rainforest preservation.

WHY EXTINCTION SHOULD CONCERN US ALL

Probably the biggest concern with extinction is the loss of the gene pool. Animals such as the rhinoceros took millions of years to evolve. It has a gene pool like no other creature on earth. When it is gone, its particular genes are gone forever. The creation of gene banks, where DNA from different animals is preserved is not a substitute for the animal itself.

If a particular plant or animal is lost to the world we may discover that it was vital to our own survival. It may have been a link in our food chain or somehow protected us from disease.

Another aspect of preservation of species is the selfish fact that many of them have given us medicines as well as food. More than ninety percent of all drugs sold over the counter originally came from wild resources.

A drug which effectively fights childhood leukemia comes from an obscure periwinkle plant found on the Island of Madagascar. A drug, taxol, found in the bark of a yew tree is effective in fighting uterine cancer in women.

We don't know how many plants and animals out there have potential for making our lives more comfortable and extending our own lifespans. If they become extinct we will never know.

FACTORS OF WILDLIFE HABITAT

Like every other living animal on earth, wild animals need food and shelter. Shelter, which is cover, protects the animal from predators, humans and adverse weather conditions.

The habitat provides the animal with food and water. Even the desert animals must get water somehow. The birds of the desert usually fly to a waterhole and immerse themselves. They fly back to the nest and shake this water loose into the open mouths of their nestlings.

Animals can survive for many days without food but only a few days without water. A person can go at least a month without food and not suffer any ill effects. A week without water makes dehydration conditions in the body almost impossible to reverse.

Territory is an area of habitat defended by a species. Establishing territory assures the species of a supply of food, an area to mate and raise young and reduce predation. It also prevents disease from moving rapidly thorough a population.

Territory needs vary greatly from species to species. A deer might stake out a square mile but a black bear needs at least forty square miles.

In creating or enhancing habitat the experimenter must keep in mind these needs of species. But it must also be kept in mind that creating habitat for one species, destroys it for another. If you create open areas for

70

9-3 A fish ladder on the Columbia River. Dams built for hydroelectricity and irrigation water storage prevent migrating fish from returning upstream to spawn. The fish ladder is an inclined water course that permits salmon and other fish to work their way to the reservoir and into the upper tributaries.

rabbits, you destroy the woodlands for squirrels.

Today, the habitats of many animals are being destroyed by urbanization , new farming practices and pollution. Acid rain has decimated many forests and caused life forms in lakes to disappear. Lead poisoning has developed in waterfowl which mistake lead shot of hunters for seeds in water. Oil pollution killed over a hundred thousand waterfowl a year in each year of the 1980s. Farming practices has filled the air with pesticides and polluted streams with fertilizers and eroded soil. We need the food but we must also insure that the production of food is carried on with preserving our environment.

Each species needs a particular habitat. We can enhance waterfowl habitat by protecting wetlands, creating openings in marshland to facilitate waterfowl movement, construct artificial ponds and swamps and construct artificial nesting islands in large water areas. The best protection afforded waterfowl has been the establishment of the National Wildlife Refuge System.

In the United States, every state has its own game and fish commission which has been entrusted with the development of state lands for preservation of wildlife. The people who operate and manage these lands have been trained in modern scientific management techniques and we can feel comfortable that at least at this level our wildlife is in good hands. However, we must guard against developers who have money and use it to influence our legislators and who have historically tried to intrude into protected habitat. Wetlands will always be a source of conflict between those who would protect them and those who would "develop" them.

10 WETLAND RESOURCES

(The following discussion is based on publications by the U.S. Fish and Wildlife Service and the U.S. Environmental Protection Agency. It pertains only to the United States)

Wetlands include the wide variety of marshes, swamps and bogs that occur throughout the country. They range from red maple swamps and black spruce bogs in the northern states to salt marshes along the coasts to bottomland hardwood forests in the southern states to prairie potholes in the Midwest to playa lakes and cottonwood willow riparian wetlands in the western states to the wet tundra.

Wetlands usually lie in depressions or along rivers, lakes and coastal waters where they are subject to periodic flooding. Some, however,

occur on slopes where they are associated with ground water seeps. Conceptually, wetlands lie between well drained upland and permanently flooded deep waters of lakes, rivers and coastal embayments (Figure 10-2). Recognizing this, one must determine where along this natural wetness continuum wetland ends and upland begins. Many wetlands form in distinct depressions or basins that can be readily observed. However, the wetland-upland boundary is not always that easy to identify. Wetlands may occur in almost imperceptibly shallow depressions and cover vast acreages. In the Prairie Pothole Region, wetland boundaries change over time due to varying rainfall patterns. In these situations, only a skilled wetland ecologist or other specialist can identify the wetland boundary

10-1 Duck boxes in a swamp. The artificial nesting site restricts predators and provides the ducklings immediate access to water. Wetlands contain more species of wildlife than any other upland ecosystem.

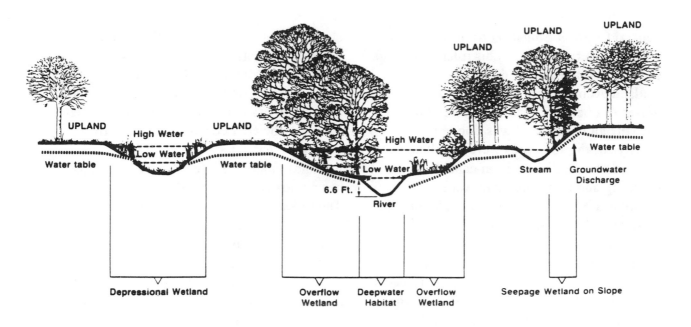

10-2 Schematic diagram showing wetlands, deepwater habitats and uplands on landscape. Note differences in wetlands due to hydrology and topographic location.

with precision.

Wetlands were historically defined by scientists working in specialized fields, such as botany or hydrology. A botanical definition would focus on the plants adapted to flooding and/or saturated soil conditions, while a hydrologist's definition would emphasize the position of the water table relative to the ground surface over time. A more complete definition of wetland involves a multidisciplinary approach. The Fish and Wildlife Service has taken this approach in developing its wetland definition and classification system.

DEFINITION OF WETLANDS

In developing an ecologically sound definition of wetland, it was acknowledged that there is no single, correct, indisputable, ecologically sound definition for wetlands, primarily because of the diversity of wetlands and because the demarcation between dry and wet environments lies along a continuum. Previous wetland definitions grew out of different needs for defining wetlands among various disciplines, e.g. wetland regulators, waterfowl managers, hydrologists, flood control engineers and water quality experts. The Fish and Wildlife Service specifically defines wetlands as follows:

"Wetlands are lands transitional between terrestrial and aquatic systems where the water table is usually at or near the surface or the land is covered by shallow water. Wetlands must have one or more of the following three attributes (1) at least periodically, the land supports predominantly hydrophytes; (2) the substrate is predominantly undrained hydric soil: and (3) the substrate is nonsoil and is saturated with water or covered by shallow water at some time during the growing season of each year".

In defining wetland from an ecological standpoint, there are three key attributes: (1) hydrology - the degree of flooding or soil saturation; (2) wetland vegetation (hydrophytes), and (3) hydric soils. All areas considered wetland must have enough water at some time during the growing season to stress plants and animals not adapted for life in water or saturated soils. Most wetlands also have hydrophytes and hydric soils present. A definition similar to this was used in

73

Federal Court in Louisiana to make a legal wetland determination. In his ruling the judge decided that the area in dispute constituted wetland according to Section 404 of the Clean Water Act because records showed that virtually all of the tract was flooded every other year, the soil types were classified as wetland soils and vegetation capable of surviving and reproducing in wetlands predominated the site. The rationale for using these three key attributes now has legal precedent.

When soils are covered by water or saturated to the surface, free oxygen is usually not available to plant roots. Most plant roots must have access to free oxygen for respiration and growth. Flooding during the growing season presents problems for growth and survival of most plants. In a wetland situation, plants must be adapted to cope with these stressful conditions. If flooding occurs only in winter when the plants are dormant, there is little or no effect on them.

Permanently flooded deepwater is not included in the definition of wetland. Instead, these waterbodies, generally deeper than six feet, are defined as deepwater habitats, since water and not air is the principal medium in which dominant organisms must live.

The Fish and Wildlife Service spent four years on developing their definition of wetland. This definition is accepted as the national and international standard for identifying wetland.

MAJOR WETLAND TYPES OF THE UNITED STATES

Wetlands occur in every state and due to regional differences in climate, vegetation, soil and hydrologic conditions, they exist in a variety of sizes, shapes and types. Wetlands can even exist in deserts.

The Fish and Wildlife Service's classification system groups wetlands according to ecologically similar characteristics. It divides wetlands and deepwater habitats into five ecological systems: (1) Marine (2) Estuarine (3) Riverine (4) Lacustrine, and (5) Palustrine. The Marine System generally consists of the open ocean and its associated coastline. It is mostly a deepwater habitat system, with marine wetlands limited to intertidal areas such as beaches, rocky shores and some coral reefs. The Estuarine System includes coastal wetlands like salt and brackish tidal marshes, mangrove swamps and intertidal flats, as well as deepwater bays, sounds and coastal rivers. The Riverine System is limited to freshwater river and stream channels and is mainly a deepwater habitat system. The Lacustrine System is also a deepwater dominated system, but includes standing waterbodies like lakes, reservoirs and deep ponds. The Palustrine System encompasses the vast majority of the country's inland marshes, bogs and swamps and does not include any deepwater habitat.

IMPORTANCE OF WETLANDS

Although often used by many people for hunting, trapping and fishing, wetlands were largely considered wasteland whose best use could only be attained through reclamation projects such as drainage for agriculture and filling for industrial or residential development. Much to the contrary, wetlands in their natural state provide a wealth of values to society. Wetland benefits can be divided into three basic categories: (1) fish and wildlife values, (2) environmental quality values, and (3) socio-economic values.

Fish and Wildlife Values
Fish and Shellfish Habitat
Waterfowl and Other Bird Habitat
Furbearer and Other Wildlife Habitat
Environmental Quality Values
Water Quality Maintenance
Pollution Filter
Sediment Removal
Oxygen Production

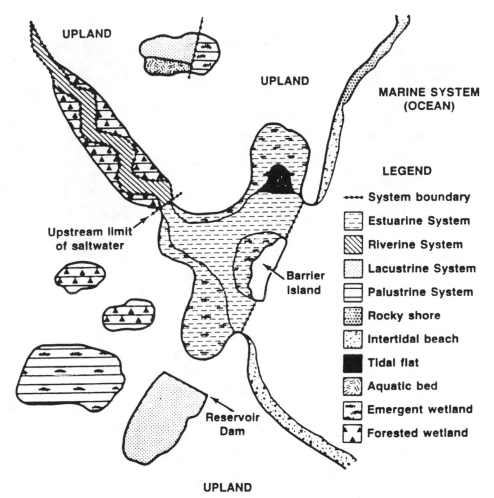

UPLAND

UPLAND

MARINE SYSTEM (OCEAN)

Upstream limit
of saltwater

Barrier
Island

Reservoir
Dam

LEGEND

- System boundary
- Estuarine System
- Riverine System
- Lacustrine System
- Palustrine System
- Rocky shore
- Intertidal beach
- Tidal flat
- Aquatic bed
- Emergent wetland
- Forested wetland

UPLAND

10-3 Diagram showing major wetland and deepwater habitat systems.

Nutrient Recycling
Chemical and Nutrient Absorption
Aquatic Productivity
Microclimate Regulator
World Climate (Ozone layer)
Socio-Economic Values
 Flood Control
Wave Damage Protection
Erosion Control
Groundwater Recharge and Water Supply
Timber and Other Natural Products
Energy Source (Peat)
Livestock Grazing
Fishing and Shellfishing
Hunting and Trapping
Recreation
Aesthetics
Education and Scientific Research

FORCES CHANGING WETLANDS

Wetlands represent a dynamic natural environment which are subjected to both human and natural forces. These forces directly result in wetland gains and losses as well as affect their quality.

Human Threats

1. Drainage for crop production, timber production and mosquito control.

2. Dredging and stream channelization for navigation channels, flood protection, coastal housing developments and reservoir maintenance.

3. Filling for dredged spoil and other solid waste disposal, roads and highways, and commercial, residential and industrial development.

10-4 A swamp in South Carolina. Wetlands, such as these, help to prevent flooding, add to underground water reserves, absorb nutrients and make a home for wildlife.

4. Construction of dikes, dams, levees and seawalls for flood control, water supply, irrigation and storm protection.

5. Discharges of materials (e.g. pesticides, herbicides, other pollutants, nutrient loading from domestic sewage and agricultural runoff and sediments from dredging and filling, agricultural and other land development) into waters and wetlands.

6. Mining of wetland soils for peat, coal, sand, gravel, phosphate and other materials.

Indirect Human Threats

1. Sediment diversion by dams, deep channels and other structures.

2. Hydrologic alterations by canals, spoil banks, roads and other structures.

3. Subsidence due to extraction of groundwater, oil, gas, sulfur and other minerals.

Natural Threats
1. Subsidence
2. including natural rise of sea   level.
3. Droughts
4. Hurricanes and other storms
5. Erosion
6. Biotic effects, e.g. muskrat, nutria and
   goose eating.

Natural events influencing wetlands include rising sea level, natural succession, the hydrologic cycle, sedimentation, erosion, beaver dam construction and fire. The rise in sea level both increases and decreases wetland acreage depending on local factors.

Human actions are particularly significant in determining the fate of wetlands. Unfortunately, many human activities are destructive to wetlands, either converting them to agricultural or other lands or degrading their quality. Key human impacts include drainage for agriculture, channelization for flood control, filling in for housing, highway and sanitary landfills, dredging for navigation channels, harbors and marinas, reservoir construction, timber harvest, peat mining, oil and gas extraction, strip mining, groundwater extraction and various forms of waste disposal.

Wetland losses and degradation continue throughout the country. There are several areas where wetlands are in greatest jeopardy from a national standpoint. These areas are (1) the estuarine wetlands of the U.S. coastal zone (2) Louisiana's coastal marshes, (3) Chesapeake Bay's submerged aquatic beds, (4) South Florida's palustrine wetlands, (5) Prairie Pothole Region's emergent wetlands, (6) wetlands of Nebraska's Sandhills and Rainwater Basin, (7) forested wetlands of the Lower Mississippi Alluvial Plain, (8) North Carolina's pocosins, and (9) western riparian wetlands. Most of these regions are under intense pressure from agricultural interests.

FUTURE OF AMERICA'S WETLANDS

The U.S. population is growing by 1.7 million each year. More than half the population lives within 50 miles of a major coast. Pressures to develop estuarine and palustrine wetlands in coastal areas will remain intense, despite the existence of laws to protect these wetlands. As the population swells in the uplands, public managers will be greatly challenged to protect wetlands from future developments.

The population move to the sunbelt states of the Southeast and Southwest will increase urban and industrial development pressures on wetlands. There will be competition for water between agriculture and non-agriculture users. Fish and wildlife will probably lose out.

The move from urban cities to suburban locations have reduced agricultural land in rural areas. These suburban counties have threatened the remaining wetlands. Since most states do not have wetland protection laws, Federal regulation through the Clean Water Act is the key means to protecting these wetlands.

Increases in world population will create a demand for American farm products and this in turn will put pressure on the protection of wetlands. This demand for American grain has already led to the conversion of vast acreages of bottomland forested wetlands to cropland in the Mississippi Alluvial Plain.

American farms are experiencing a decline in returns per unit of product and this forces farmers to increase production in order to maintain the same level of income. Since much prime farmland has been converted to non-agricultural uses there has been a tendency to make up for this by conversion of rangelands and wetlands to cropland. The use of irrigation by lowering water tables has increased the destruction of wetlands, especially in the West.

Agriculture has always played a role in

degrading water quality, fish and wildlife habitat and the quality of wetlands. About 68% of all water pollution in the U.S. is caused by agriculture, with soil erosion from cropland being the single greatest contributor to stream sediment. Improved soil management practices are of utmost importance on present farmland.

Wetland protection can be accomplished by acquisition of wetlands and regulation of wetland uses. The use of tax incentives to encourage preservation of wetlands by landowners represents a potentially valuable tool in protecting wetlands. The removal of government subsidies which encourages wetland destruction would also benefit wetlands greatly.

The acquisition of wetlands for migratory birds has been especially successful in protecting them. These have been acquired under The Migratory Bird Conservation Act of 1929, The Migratory Bird Hunting and Conservation Stamp Act of 1934, and the Land and Water Conservation Fund Act. Landowners can receive reimbursement through the Soil Conservation Service's Water Bank Program.

Federal funds and state governments cannot be expected to protect all of our wetlands. However, wetland regulations at the Federal and state levels are vital to preserving our wetlands and saving the public values they provide.

Property Rights vs The Common Good

In the United States we are used to thinking in terms of "individual freedom and rights". Asian cultures think in terms of the rights of the community or society taking precedent over those of an individual. In some instances, we put the welfare of society above that of the individual when we condemn property for such uses as schools, highways, hospitals or for national defense.

As our population increases there will be more demand for food, homes, roads and schools. We will be forced to make decisions concerning which lands to preserve and which will be used to supply those necessities. The problem reaches emotional heights when people who own wetlands want to destroy them and convert them to economic uses. Most people who want less government regulation on the use of their land belong to groups identified as "Wise Use" groups. These groups are particularly offended by the wetland regulations which prevent them from draining or filling in the wetlands on their "private property".

Property rights involve entitlements, privileges and limitations which define the owner's right to use a resource, in this case the property. Wetlands are particularly vulnerable since many of them are in high use areas. Coastal wetlands are prime recreation and condominium properties. Prairie wetlands are in prime farm areas. Almost all wetlands are vulnerable to development.

Destruction of one acre of wetland may have little impact on a watershed but when many one acre plots are destroyed it has serious environmental implications. When we legislate to keep people from using their property, in this case wetlands, aren't we in effect condemning the property for the good of society. So, where do individual property rights end and society's resource rights begin?

Cities 100% Dependent on Ground Water

Albuquerque	Orlando
Baton Rouge	Riverside
Dayton	San Antonio
Ft. Lauderdale	St. Petersburg
Jacksonville	Tucson

The per capita use of water is highest in Tacoma where citizens use 691 gallons a day. The next highest per capita use cities are Atlanta 472, Wilmington DE 419, Baltimore 342, Ft. Lauderdale 330 and Dayton 318.

11 MARINE RESOURCES

Humans are intimately tied to the ocean ecosystem. We get food from the waters and we use them for transportation. They produce fresh water for the hydrologic process and their green plants provide the earth with oxygen in the process of photosynthesis.

The ocean occupies approximately seventy percent of the earth's surface. Its deepest trenches reach down to six and a half miles. The average salt content of the ocean is three and a half percent. If you boiled off one hundred pounds of sea water you would get three and a half pounds of salt.

Current flow and upwelling are two movements of the ocean water that impact the life forms in the ocean. Warm currents move from the equator toward the poles and cold currents move from the poles toward the equator. They each have specific life forms which depend on them. Upwelling occurs in distinct areas depending on the rotation of the earth and the configuration of the ocean floor. Strong upwelling off the western coast of South America is responsible for the abundant anchovies and sardines of the area which depend on nutrients brought up from great depths.

For purposes of study, the ocean is divided into various zones based on physical properties. The littoral zone is the beach where low and high tides operate. Beaches may be sand but the majority of them are composed of stones and gravel.

The edges of the continents extend out into the ocean and these continental shelf zones are referred to as neritic. From here the ocean slopes down to the deep. This slope or bathyal zone begins at about 200 meters and ends at about 2000 meters where the abyssal zone or ocean deep begins.

The open ocean is referred to as pelagic and the ocean bottom is benthic. The area where sunlight penetrates is the photic or euphotic zone. Generally the red wave lengths penetrate to 30 meters and the violet to 300.

Various landforms are found in the open ocean. These include ridges which mark the boundaries between the earth plates. The Mid-Atlantic Ridge stretches from Iceland down to southern reaches parallel to the tips of Africa and South America.

Isolated mountain peaks under water are known as sea mounts. When waves have eroded them and made them flat topped they are called guyots after the man who first identified them.

Island arcs and deep trenches appear where one earth plate is slipping under another. These can be seen by studying a map of the western Pacific Ocean.

Coral builds up many landforms. When next to a landmass they form fringing reefs and offshore they form barrier reefs. When coral takes a circular shape it forms islands with a central lagoon. These are known as atolls.

There are also many sea canyons around the world. These appear to be extensions of river valleys on land. Perhaps these formed when glaciers tied up much of the world's water during the Ice Ages.

ESTUARIES

The ocean feature with the greatest impact on most humans are the estuaries. These are large indentations in the coastline where fresh water carried by rivers meets salt water of the ocean. One of the largest estuaries in the world is Chesapeake Bay.

During high tide, salt water predominates in the estuary. When low tide occurs, fresh water is at its maximum. Generally the saline content of the estuary runs between 1.0 and 3.0 with an average about 1.8. Animals such as oysters, clams, crabs and shrimp seem to prefer this salinity.

Since the water level rises and falls with the tides a unique ecosystem develops on the shorelines of the estuary. The animals here learn to duck in and out of the water or survive by going without water for a period of time. Many, such as clams, adapt by burying themselves in the beach until the water returns.

The combination of tides and river flows causes a turbidity to develop in the estuary. This clouding action limits the development of phytoplankton but nutrient levels are kept high due to the incoming tides and the river flow.

More than sixty percent of all seafood harvested by American fishermen spends most of its time in the estuary. The estuary also provides food and breeding sites for millions of waterfowl and fur-bearing mammals.

The wetlands connected with estuaries are full of water at high tide but they still provide a natural filtering system for many types of human pollution. Fifteen acres of estuary wetlands provide the filtering system equal to a city the size of Syracuse, New York.

The coastal wetlands associated with estuaries absorb the shock of ocean waves during severe storms such as hurricanes. This prevents erosion. For this reason we should not destroy wetlands surrounding the estuaries by building on them.

NEGATIVE IMPACTS ON OCEAN LIFE

A creature living in the ocean has many adverse influences on it. Surviving to adulthood is a real struggle for most species. For instance, out of a million clam larvae only two will survive to adulthood and be able to reproduce. Thus the clam survives as a species by overpopulation of the environment. The overpopulation feeds many other species.

Predators probably wipe out more individuals than any other negative aspect of the ocean. Predators not only include fish that feed on other fish but thousands of terns, gulls, cormorants, pelicans and other sea birds that feed directly on fish. Every sea creature has its predators including the mighty whale whose main predator is human.

Snails, starfish and coral are among the most voracious predators. The shark gets all the publicity for preying on humans in the ocean but the marine crocodile kills more people in a year.

Basically the food chain starts out with phytoplankton, the floating plant matter. This is consumed by zooplankton, the small animals which float along with the phytoplankton. The zooplankton is then consumed by larger sea life such as fish and these are consumed by the fish-eating predators such as barracuda, salmon, shark and cod which may eventually be consumed by the ultimate predator-humans.

Second in the destruction of sea life are the parasites and disease causing organisms. We are, of course, looking at the situation from the view point of humans. The disease causing organisms and parasites are a part of the earth ecosystem and worthy of survival in their own right.

Diseases and parasites of sea creatures involve protozoans, bacteria, fungi, flukes, roundworms, flatworms and lampreys. Parasites such as the tapeworm make it hazardous to consume raw fish. The lamprey is an eel-like fish with a round mouth full of sharp teeth. With these teeth and sucker mouth the lamprey attaches itself to the side of a fish and sucks out its fluids. When the lamprey invaded the Great Lakes it decimated the lake trout, one of the lakes most popular food fish. Fish managers have learned to control the lamprey on the Great Lakes by using electric shocking techniques and poisons in the fresh water streams where the lamprey larva are born.

The Red Tide organisms are caused by dinoflagellates, a marine protozoan. These turn sea water reddish-born and hence the name red tide. The red tide organisms release a toxic chemical which kills fish and

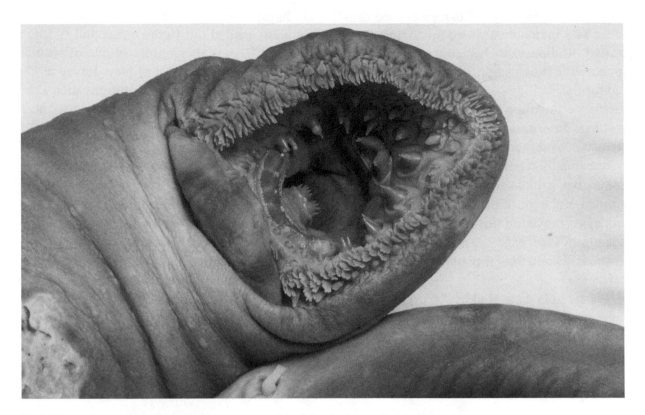

11-1 The sucker mouth of the lamprey, a parasitic fish which attaches itself to the side of other fish, bores a hole and sucks its blood and other fluids.

eventually the predator which eats the fish. Red tide also kills by depleting oxygen in an area.

Sewage and sludge dumping has always been a hazard to ocean life. Because the waste depletes oxygen it has a high mortality rate in the region of dumping. The sludge also release high amounts of heavy metals such as chromium and lead which damages fish by killing them directly or causing mutations in their offspring.

The National Oceanic and Atmospheric Administration has identified five critical areas of sewage and sludge dumping off the United States shores. These are around New York City, Boston Harbor, Salem Harbor of Massachusetts, Raritan Bay of New Jersey and the coastal shelf off San Diego.

The United States banned ocean dumping of sewage and sludge as of January 1, 1992.

However, many cities violate this ban and there seems to be no enforcement of its dictates. Until the ban was enacted New York City dumped an estimated weight of four million tons of sewage into the ocean each year.

The release of hot water from cleaning out boilers of the electric industry also is detrimental to sea life. Water at 212 degrees Fahrenheit is released into the ocean by thousands of boilers weekly. These kill fish in the immediate area and may kill organisms as far as four hundred feet offshore. Most fish along the Atlantic seacoast live in waters at less than sixty degrees and are killed even at temperatures of ninety degrees.

Using the ocean as a dumping ground for radioactive wastes has been a practice since the creation of excess wastes from the military and electrical industry. Despite regulations and international treaties, many countries and especially Russia has used the ocean as a radioactive waste dumping ground. Radioactivity has consistently appeared in tuna caught off the coast of California.

Plastic pollution is a serious ocean problem. Enormous volumes of plastic ride the waves and there are no organizations systematically removing these from the ocean. Some civic groups clean up the beaches each summer and a lot of plastic that washes up on shore is removed in this manner. In one cleanup of the Texas coast more than 32,000 plastic bags and 31,000 plastic bottles were removed.

Plastic nets discarded by fishermen are a continuous hazard. Once the nets are in the ocean they form a "ghost fleet" that goes about still catching fish, porpoises, seals and sea birds. Once entangled in the nets there is no escape and no harvest.

In many areas of the world, garbage is regularly hauled out to the ocean and dumped. This is also a great source of plastic. Fish caught off the coast of New Jersey in one scientific study contained items such as cigarette butts, bandages and plastic toys in their stomachs.

OIL POLLUTION

Nothing is more dramatic or gets more attention from the news media than an oil tanker mishap and the resulting oil pollution. However dramatic, tanker mishaps are only a small part of the oil pollution problem. Today, most countries have laws regulating the construction of tankers and most of them are double-hulled. Some countries such as Liberia and Panama permit tankers to fly their flags with no regulations or inspections.

Oil pollution comes not only from tanker accidents but from offshore drilling and transportation of oil, leaks in oil pipelines,

11-2 Crab traps piled on a wharf in Alaska. Crabs are one of the leading ocean catch species of the United States fishing fleet.

atmospheric transportation of airborne hydrocarbons, waste crankcase oil, coastal refineries and natural leaks in the ocean floor where oil seeps out.

By far the biggest source of ocean oil pollution comes from the inadequate disposal of crankcase oil. Since this problem has been well documented most industrialized nations have regulations regarding the disposal of this waste oil. Much of it will be recycled in the future.

Oil pollution causes a reduction in photosynthesis and this in turn affects the food chain by the decrease in production of phytoplankton. It also affects oxygen production of green plants and has some effect then on atmospheric oxygen.

Once the oyster and clam beds have been polluted with oil they are no longer suitable for human consumption. This is true of most marine animals we use for food.

Oil pollution kills marine birds and mammals by coating their bodies and preventing natural air layers within their outer coverings to function properly.

Almost all the birds, seals and otters saved in the big oil spills off San Diego and in the Alaskan Gulf eventually died when released back to the natural environment.

Oil pollution interferes with the natural communication of mammals such as whales and porpoises. This has been documented but needs further study. We really don't know what the effects of the disrupted communication has on the animals life.

Finally, the oil pollution concentrates chlorinated hydrocarbons which make up the bulk of pesticides. The pesticides such as DDT, toxaphene and aldrin are washed into the ocean and are dissolved by oil. This makes it easier for these poisons to enter the food chain. Polychlorinated biphenals (PCBs) used extensively in the electrical industry are also soluble in oil.

HARVESTING FISH AND OTHER SEA CREATURES

Circular nets or purse seines are the most used method of commercial fishing. These are large nets strung out in a circle and once sufficient time for fish to accumulate in them has elapsed the strings are drawn and the circle is brought in. Some of these nets are a mile long and weigh sixteen tons. These, of course, must be handled with machinery and not by hand.

Trawling involves baited hooks or nets dragged behind a moving boat. Trawling nets are excellent methods of catching cod, herring, flounder and haddock. Trawling hooks are used mostly in sport fishing.

Gill nets are long walls of nets set with floats at the top and weights at the bottom. These are put out at night and gathered in the day. Fish are caught by putting their heads into the weave of the net and when they can't withdraw because of their gill movements they are caught. This is an excellent method of harvesting large schools of fish. The size of the fish caught is regulated by the size of the net opening.

Harpooning is used to capture large mammals such as whales and seals. The harpoon spear is shot out of a cannon and once embedded in the prey, explodes, killing it.

Most fish caught in the ocean by American fishermen are frozen. This accounts for about one fourth of the total yearly catch. Fresh fish accounts for about a fifth of the fish sold in American markets. Canning accounts for a little over ten percent of the market. Other methods of preserving and marketing involve drying, salting, pickling and chemical preservation.

OVERHARVESTING OF OCEAN CREATURES

Since 1960 the great fishing grounds off the coast of Newfoundland, Iceland and Norway have been devoid of desirable

11-3 Hand stripping eggs from a female walleye. The eggs will be fertilized with milt from a male fish. After the young hatch and grow to two inches they will be released into the wild.

species of fish such as cod, haddock, perch and hake. The Worldwatch Institute which monitors world food has documented that the top year for ocean catch was in 1990 when slightly over a hundred million tons of ocean food was harvested. In the next three years the catch has dwindled by three million tons and by 1993 the catch was put at 91 million tons. They expect this supply to dwindle slowly into the future.

In order of dollar value the most desirable product of the seas for the United States has been shrimp. This is followed in order by salmon, tuna, clams, crabs, menhaden, oysters, cod, haddock and scallops. Shrimp stocks around the world are being depleted. In order to satisfy the world appetite for shrimp the harvest goes on around the clock. Some progress has been made in shrimp farming and this may be the key to shrimp futures.

The fishing nations which account for more than five percent of the world harvest each year include (in order of tonnage caught) Japan, Russia, China, Chile, United States and Peru. Other nations with large fishing fleets include the United Kingdom, Norway, Iceland, Portugal and Spain.

Various schemes are used to improve fishing in the oceans. Many countries such as the United States raise anadromous fish in nurseries and release them. These are fish that breed in fresh water and go out to salt water to live and return to fresh water again to spawn. These include salmon, shad and smelt. American fishermen resent the Japanese who do not raise salmon but wait offshore of areas like the Columbia River for the spawning run and take large harvests of salmon once reared in American nurseries.

Fish reproduction can also be encouraged by building artificial reefs offshore. These may be made from mounds of old automobile tires to the carcasses of automobiles. These reefs encourage algae to form and this in turn gives fish protection as well as food.

Regulations of fishing is the best method of insuring an adequate fish supply for the future. Various commissions have instituted fishing seasons, size limits, number of pound limits and species limits. However, there is no international organization with authority to enforce these suggested regulations and no penalties for violators. Many countries have signed the charges suggested by organizations such as the International Whaling Commission (IWC) and most who have signed have obeyed the suggested regulations. However, countries such as Japan and Russia do not agree to these commission regulations. In 1995, Japan, Russia, Iceland and Norway refused to sign the IWC's charter on whaling.

Seafood makes up the single largest source of animal protein in the world, more than beef, chicken, sheep, or pork. More than twenty percent of the world's population depend on fish as their only source of protein. Those numbers depending on fish for protein keep expanding but the fish catch keeps decreasing.

The world fishing crises has several negative aspects. These include (1) habitat destruction, especially of coastal waters where most fish spawn, (2) destruction of mangrove forests, another spawning and nursery habitat, (3) destruction of coral reefs, (4) destruction of estuaries, (5) pollution which keeps fish from reproducing and locating prey, (6) global climate changes, (7) relocation of alien species such as the zebra mussel and (8) inadequate scientific knowledge about management techniques.

Almost 90 percent of the world fish exports are purchased by the United States, Japan and countries of Europe. Most of this is imported from Lesser Developed Countries that could use the catch for their own nutritional needs.

Many countries do not have adequate control of their fishing fleets and therefore cannot enforce regulations such as fish size, numbers, annual catch and harvest techniques. Fishing fleets do not wish to regulate themselves.

If there is lack of regulation in the Lesser Developed Countries then it can be said that the regulations of the developed countries are influenced by the political pressure of those engaged in fishing. This permits harvesting of the ocean beyond sustainable levels when fish stocks are obviously declining.

As the population increases and there is more demand for sea products, governments will have to cooperate in regulating the harvest or the resource will be in complete chaos. This will result in starvation in many countries that rely on fish for their suvival.

Our Coral Reefs are Dying

Coral reefs are the largest structures made by living creatures. They are the skeletal remains of tiny, tentacled coral polyps that feed on plankton. The polyps are among the most ancient forms of life on the planet. Coral reefs support a variety of life equal to that of the tropical rainforest.

Threats to coral reefs include sediments from dredging operations, sediments from deforestation, industrial chemicals, pesticides from agriculture, oil spills, illegal use of dynamite in fishing, abrasion from boats and anchors and harvesting coral for aquariums.

Natural disturbances of coral include algol blooms, infestations of "thorn-of-crowns" starfish and warming of sea water.

MAJOR OCEAN FISHING AREAS AND PERCENTAGE OF CATCH, 1995

Bering Sea to Japan	35
England to Iceland	16
Peru - Chile coastline	11
North of New Guinea	9
Madeira to Canary Is.	5

12 MINERAL RESOURCES

There are several definitions for the term mineral. The geologist might define a mineral as an inorganic substance occurring naturally in the earth and having distinctive physical properties and a composition that can be expressed by a chemical formula. A geographer might define a mineral as any substance extracted from the earth having economic value or use. A nutritionist might talk about vitamins and minerals. For our purposes we shall define a mineral as any substance that is neither animal or vegetable, that is, nonliving.

Economists classify minerals according to their content and use. The following system is one example of classification.

I. METALS	II. NONMETALS
A. Ferro-alloys	A. Fertilizers
B. Common metals	B. Building stone
C. Rare metals	C. Fuels

Minerals are nonrenewable. Once gone, they cannot be made to come back. They are a limited resource. Except for the fuels, minerals can be partially recycled which will put off the day when they will no longer be available for human use.

Most minerals are extracted from the surface or just below the surface of the earth. Most exist as chemical compounds consisting of a metal and some other substance, such as iron oxide. These are also encased in some rock that must be discarded in the preparation of minerals for human use. This rock is called an ore. To get at the iron the rock must be crushed and heated or treated with chemicals. When a deposit is of economic importance it is called an ore deposit. For an ore to be exploited the mineral sought must be of economic value greater than the value expended to get it. Therefore it must be a deposit of some volume. It must be close enough to the surface to be mined conomically. It must have a certain grade, that is a concentration great enough to make extracting it feasible. Another requirement is that the location of the deposit be accessible and near the market where it will be used if it is of considerabale weight.

THE UNITED STATES AND ITS USE OF METALS

The United States has about five percent of the world's population and uses about thirty five percent of world's metal resources. If we tried to bring the rest of the world up to the standard of living of the United States it could not be done. In order to improve the standard of living of the rest of the world the United States will have to reduce its own.

Probably the most evident sign of opulence in the United States is the automobile. There is one vehicle for every person in the country. As a result, we junk over seven million automobiles a year and produce more than 250 million used tires. To produce our automobiles we use eight percent of all our copper, ten percent of aluminum, fourteen percent of nickel, twenty percent of steel , thirty five percent of zinc, and slightly more than half of the nation's lead. What this means is that of all the copper used in the United States each year, eight percent of it is used in producing automobiles. If we found some way of reducing the number of automobiles we could save an enormous amount of minerals.

A disturbing fact of economics is that the United States is not independent when it comes to metallic minerals. We import more than half of our very vital minerals. These are strategic resources and they are valuable to our military effort and to our individual health.

We import one hundred percent of all the arsenic we use as well as the bauxite, columbium, graphite, manganese, mica in sheets, strontium and yitrium. Columbium is used in the aerospace industry, manganese is the main alloy used in producing hard steel,

UNITED STATES DEPENDENCY ON IMPORTS OF MINERALS (*World Almanac*)

Mineral		U.S. Supplier	Major Use
Bauxite	100	Australia, Guinea	aluminum, aerospace
Columbium	100	Brazil, China	aerospace, alloys
Graphite	100	Mexico, China	metallurgical uses
Manganese	100	S. Africa, France	steel making
Mica sheets	100	India, Belgium	electronics
Strontium	100	Mexico	TV picture tubes
Ind. diamonds	98	Ireland, Britain	grinding, cutting
Fluorospar	89	Mexico, China	acid production
Platinum	88	S. Africa, Britain	catalytic converters
Tantalum	86	Germany, Australia	electronic parts
Tungsten	84	China, Bolivia	lamps, lighting
Chromium	82	S. Africa, Turkey	steel, chemicals
Tin	81	Brazil, Bolivia	cans, electrical
Cobalt	75	Zambia, Zaire	aerospace alloys
Potash	71	Canada, Israel	fertilizer
Cadmium	66	Canada, Mexico	batteries, plating
Nickel	64	Canada, Norway	stainless steel
Barite	58	China, India	oil drilling, fluids
Silver	57	Mexico, Canada	photography, electrical

mica is used in electronics, strontium is used in making TV picture tubes and arsenic is used in a hundred processes from pesticides to glass making.

We import more than eighty percent of our platinum, tungsten, chromium, fluorospar, tin, industrial diamonds and tantalum. We import more than seventy percent of our potash and cobalt. We import more than half our silver, antimony, nickel, barite, cadmium and zinc. We are dependent upon other countries for our supply of much of our most basic minerals.

THE FERRO-ALLOYS

Ferro-alloys are minerals mixed with iron to give it more desirable qualities. When iron was first used it was "cast iron", that is, iron poured into molds and cast into usable objects like railroad rails and plows. These broke easily. Today we still make items such as stoves and cooking pots out of cast iron.

When it was discovered that iron could be made into more durable items by adding manganese to it a new industry was born , the steel industry. Steel is iron mixed with some other metal. This permitted steel to be rolled, molded, cut, drawn into wires, and easily welded. Holes could be drilled into it and thus it can be used in making sky scrapers and bridges.

When chromium is added to steel it become stainless steel. This is used in a variety of products ranging from expensive bumpers on automobiles to hospital equipment which can be easily cleaned and will not rust. We import most of our chromium from South Africa and Zimbabwe.

Adding vanadium to steel makes it hard and when used in knives and other cutlery it can take on a sharp cutting edge. Adding tungsten gives it toughness and this steel is used in the scoops of power shovels and the

12-1 Limestone quarry in the tightly folded Nitanny Mountains of Pennsylvania. The boom swings a steel cable with a large weight against the rock face. Broken rock falls to the quarry floor and is loaded into trucks and taken to a heating and crushing operation.

blades of bull dozers. Cobalt steel is used in the aerospace industry.

OTHER METALS

Most other metals do not need alloying for the uses that society makes of them. Aluminum is the second metal of use in the world. It is mined as an ore called bauxite. Bauxite is pulverized and the aluminum oxide is separated from it and concentrated by many mechanical processes. This concentrated ore is known as alumina. Shipping alumina is cheaper in the long run than shipping the entire ore. The alumina is then subjected to electrolysis and refined into aluminum. This takes huge amounts of electricity and therefore aluminum industries are usually located in areas of hydroelectric plants where cheap electricity is available.

Other metals widely used which the United States produces in abundance are copper, lead and molybdenum. Can you name at least five other metals that haven't been mentioned so far in this chapter?

FERTILIZERS AND BUILDING STONE

When we consider the importance of metals, fertilizers and building stone to our lifestyles we begin to see that there might be a future crises as these are used up. About fifty percent of our crop production is based on the use of fertilizers. Presently the fertilizer resource is based on phosphate rock, nitrates and potash. Nitrates can be created from using the air which is 78 percent nitrogen, although this requires large amounts of energy. However, the phosphate and potash rock are slowly being diminished to a critical state. We simply do not have enough of these valuable fertilizer rocks to keep up with the expanding world population and the need to produce more food.

There is an abundance of building materials everywhere on earth. In the United States we have plenty of sand, gravel, clay, and limestone which is the basis for the cement and concrete industries. We are abundant in granite, sandstone, gneiss and marble for building.

The clay industry is often overlooked in our use of minerals. We use clay in ceramics, making bricks, bathroom fixtures and tile for pipes and roofing.

ARE WE RUNNING OUT OF MINERALS?

How long will the present supply of minerals last? Of course, each mineral must be calculated separately. We must figure in the amount of reserves, the present use of the mineral and the anticipated future use. Some future uses cannot be anticipated. For instance, uranium was hardly used until it was discovered that a small fraction of it was radioactive and could be used in nuclear reactors. This prompted a worldwide search for this once neglected mineral.

Even though a mineral might be abundant in the earth's crust it may not be feasible to mine it. There may not be sufficient ore deposits. For instance, aluminum is one of the most abundant metals on earth. But unless it appears in sufficient concentration it is not feasible to mine and use it.

Based on reserve estimates most of the eighty or so minerals the world depends upon are in good supply for many years to come. However, in the next fifty years we will probably have about twenty of these fall into critically short supply.

We must bear in mind that a large portion of the earth has not been explored for mineral deposits. Many remote parts of Africa, South America and Asia might turn up important minerals. However, even if we expand the present base of many minerals they are being depleted at such a rapid rate that new discoveries would have to increase

12-2 An open pit copper mine near Butte, Montana.

12-3 This coal processing plant is on the Monongahela River in Pennsylvania. Coal is mined directly from the Pittsburgh Seam in the hillside. It is washed, crushed and graded in the series of buildings. Coal mine waste is transported to the top of the hill for disposal. The graded coal is shipped by river barge to Pittsburgh where it is used to produce electricity and coke for the steel industry.

them by a factor of ten to create optimism.

Seawater contains just about every mineral found in the earth's crust. These are usually in such small amounts that extracting them is almost impossible with present technology. We can at present extract magnesium, sodium and various salts of chloride, sulfate, and carbonate profitably. We also gather manganese nodules from the ocean floor.

New extraction technologies might work for seawater and they might work for deeply buried minerals or minerals of low concentration. These technologies are not yet developed and we must assume that they will be developed but for the present we must rely on the estimates of reserves and the present rate of consumption.

With new technology or with new desperation we might go back and rework the low-grade ores or rework the mine wastes of ores of yesterday. Presently we rely on copper ore which is two percent copper. In the future we might go back to the old copper mine dumps and start reworking the waste which has an ore content of one percent or less.

One promise for the future is finding substitutes for metals. Plastics is a good alternative but future plastic supplies might be limited since most are made from petroleum. In many instances we can substitute abundant metals such as aluminum for less abundant metals such as magnesium. And we can substitute magnesium for less abundant zinc, especially in products such as paint and some chemicals.

Our best maneuver is to reduce the demand for some minerals and recycle all minerals where possible. By recycling we save energy, reduce the need for landfill space, and put off the day when we run out of specific minerals.

By recycling we save tremendous amounts of energy and save the environmental degradation of land from mining and transporting ores. Recycling one aluminum can saves the energy equivalent to a half quart of oil. It is ninety six percent cheaper to make a can from recycled aluminum than to make it from the ore.

By reusing products until they actually wear out we can also save energy and save the landfill space. By keeping automobiles repaired and out of the junk heap we can save tremendous resources. We have to resist the pressures put upon us by those who make a profit from the throw-away society.

Usually 1988 is given as a base year for estimates of reserves and consumption. At the 1988 rate, the following world mineral reserves are expected to be exhausted in the following number of years: aluminum 225, iron 167, nickel 65, copper 41, cadmium 27, lead 22, mercury 22, zinc 21 and tin 21.   In the case of petroleum, the world has about 1092 billion barrels in reserve and we are pumping about 60 million barrels a day. At this rate of extraction the world's oil supply should last about 46 years (from 1988). This is enough time to develop energy sources alternate to oil and leave the limited oil supplies to future chemical and industrial uses.

We must investigate and expand the potential for little used energy sources such as solar power, hydropower, tides, ocean waves, inland solar ponds, wind, thermal sources and biomass. The biomass includes waste wood, manure, alcohol production and use of green plants.

UNITED STATES MINERAL DILEMMA

The United States has large reserves of uranium, lead, zinc, gold, silver, nickel and copper. We also have great production of sulfur, potash and phosphate which are important to the chemical and fertilizer industries. However, we are lacking in tin, bauxite, manganese and many important ferro-alloys.

Our mineral resources are being depleted at a rapid rate. It is the exploitation of these resources which has placed the citizens of the United States among the most affluent in the world.

Since much of the high grade ore of the United States is depleted, greater emphasis is placed on imported raw materials from less affluent countries. The benefits to the raw material producing countries do not equal the loss of their resources and they realize this. As the raw material producing countries become industrialized they will begin to use their own materials for finished products thus limiting the need for our manufactured goods.

Exploiting our own minerals such as coal and copper causes environmental degradation. Since coal is abundant in North America it will continue to be a major industrial fuel. The mining, transportation and burning of coal wrecks havoc in the environment. We can minimize environmental degradation from mineral exploitation but the cost of such minimization must be weighed against the benefits. Thus it is with all minerals.

Most of the cheap minerals of North America and the world have already been exploited. Industrial countries are now going after deeper and less accessible minerals. At this time, the world is leaving an age of surplus and entering into a world of scarcity. Much of the important mineral deposits have been identified and recorded. The prospect of finding new large easily exploited important mineral deposits is slim. The world is not creating any more minerals and we have to deal with this reality.

We will soon be making a transition from wasteful mineral use to enforced conservation. Recycling will become a

12-4 A coal mine waste dump. The waste coal and shale ignites by spontaneous combustion. The result is a burnt waste called "red dog" which is used in surfacing rural roads. This dump is almost completely removed. Mining accounts for three forths of all U.S. landfill material.

necessity rather than the haphazard enterprise of today. Costs are already exhorbitent for most minerals and increasing daily. In the last twenty years the price of petroleum , gold and silver increased by a factor of 25. Increased efforts to provide more of these resources caused the price to drop to a factor of 16 in 1995 but this drop in price is only temporary only because the exploitation of these limited resources has been greatly accelerated.

In order to maintain our standard of living the United States imports approximately 20 tons of minerals each year per person. We have achieved our standard of living by exploiting our own resources at a fantastic rate. Now that our resources are dwindling we have to expand our resource base in the rest of the world. We will never again be self-sufficient and our standard of living depends largely on the world political situation.

Our government collects and stockpiles many "strategic" minerals. These are vital minerals used for military, health and economic purposes. Many industries want to cut into these stockpiles since the prospect of going to war or the depletion of the mineral sources is not likely to occur in the near future. This proposal must be considered carefully since our government has a tendency to sell stockpile and other resources below market value. We must insure that depleted supplies will be replenished.

The United States has also kept the standard of living high by running up a huge national debt. As our debt continues to increase we will be unable to buy the minerals we need from foreign sources since the value of our money will be depreciated. We cannot continue to pay other countries and mineral producers with money that isn't there. Therefore, our access to the world mineral market will be limited.

13 ENERGY RESOURCES

Every individual needs to use fuel of some sort to carry on the basic necessities of life. Even in the tropics food must be cooked on a daily basis and in most areas of the world we must have some sort of heat to keep warm.

Fuel is just one source of energy which is defined as the ability to do work. Energy of one sort or another is necessary for an industrialized world.

There are five basic fuels used in the world. These are coal, petroleum, natural gas, wood and nuclear materials. The first three, coal, petroleum and natural gas are referred to as fossil fuels since these are created from organic matter buried millions of years ago. These are the premier sources of energy since they are comparatively inexpensive and produce a lot of energy per unit of weight. These are nonrenewable resources.

COAL

Coal was formed by ancient plants buried in the sediments of the geologic past. These were once great forests which sank under the sea and were later buried by sand, mud and gravel.

Accumulated vegetation which has not undergone the pressure and time of coal is peat. This is compressed plant matter which can be cut and transported in blocks and burns readily. Several countries of the world depend heavily upon peat as a source of home fuel. Among these are Ireland, Estonia and Lithuania.

The beginnings of coal occurs when vegetation has undergone some form of change due to pressure upon it. Many of the volatiles, gases of the vegetation, are driven off and the carbon in the plant material is concentrated. When the concentration of carbon reaches about thirty percent the material is called brown coal or lignite. The United States has extensive lignite deposits in the Rocky Mountain states from Arizona and New Mexico in the south to Montana and North Dakota in the north.

Lignite is a sedimentary rock. When it is subjected to more pressure and given more time to age it becomes bituminous or soft coal. This is the most desired type of coal and it is used extensively in the iron and steel industry and to produce electric power. Lignite and bituminous coal account for 56 percent of all the electric power produced in the United States. We have large bituminous coal deposits in the Appalachian Plateau, the Illinois Basin, Michigan and a large field from Iowa to Texas. The carbon content of soft coal runs anywhere from 70 to 86 percent.

When the sedimentary coal is compressed and undergoes geologic metamorphism it becomes anthracite or hard coal. In anthracite the carbon content reaches 96 percent and it burns with a bright blue flame once it is ignited. Anthracite deposits are found in eastern Pennsylvania, Rhode Island and western Virginia.

Coal is obtained by strip mining and by deep surface mines. In strip mining the top layers of earth and rock are removed with the aid of power shovels. In large operations this overburden is removed with huge shovels called draglines. These can remove almost ten tons of overburden with one scoop. Of course this takes a lot of energy and unless the coal is at a shallow depth it is not economically feasible to remove the overburden with these expensive methods.

Strip mining tears up the land and causes much damage to nearby streams. The Surface Mining Control and Reclamation Act of 1977 required all strip mining companies to restore land to its original contour and to replant it after the operation. Many companies have found that it is cheaper to pay the imposed fine than to spend time reclaiming the land.

Shaft mining involves a large elevator shaft

13-1 Strip mining coal from a shallow deposit. The farm land pictured here was completely destroyed as mining operations expanded.

which transports men and materials into the ground to the level of the coal seam. In level mines the diggers operate machinery with ease. However, in a slope mine there are many dangers. Shaft miners are ever watchful for the build-up of poisonous methane gas which can kill them. An accumulation of methane is also subject to explosion and many miners in this country have been killed by mine explosions and trapped by cave-ins which occur with these explosions.

Shaft miners remove much material such as slate and shale which comes with the coal. This waste material is sent to the surface in small rail cars and dumped on the land. These create eyesores and are one of the biggest ingredients in landfills.

All deep mines have water accumulation and this must be pumped out if miners are to operate safely. This water plus the water which normally runs through coal seams is acid in nature.

The streams into which they flow are devoid of life and the water is an orange-brown color. Once a mine is abandoned some of the water can be contained and treated as it leaves the mine but this has proven to be a difficult task.

The United States has the largest coal reserves in the world, 29%, followed by Russia 24% and China 11%. At the present rate of consumption the world coal resources will last well over two hundred years.

Coal can be converted into a gasoline type product known as Synfuel. It can also be gasified and used in the manner of natural gas. In some deep and unaccessible deposits the coal bed can be burned and hydrogen, carbon monoxide and methane released can be

13-2 An offshore oil rig. Offshore drilling pollutes the ocean with oil but most ocean oil pollution comes from activities on land.

captured and used. But all of these are currently more expensive than using petroleum and natural gas.

PETROLEUM

Most people refer to petroleum as oil and we shall do that also. For centuries oil was found in surface seeps and on water and used to light smoky lamps. When it was discovered that kerosene, a brightly burning product could be made from oil a search for new ways to obtain oil was underway. Edwin Drake was able to get significant amounts of oil by drilling a well through pipe casing. His successful well at Titusville, Pennsylvania in 1859 launched the oil industry as we know it today.

Oil is a liquid which is easy to transport and store. Most of it moves by pipeline on land and by ocean tanker from land to land. It is much cleaner burning than coal and there is no ash waste left for disposal.

Oil can be broken down into many products such as gasoline, kerosene, and heating oil. It is the mainstay of the plastics industry. The main use of oil is in transportation, running the vehicles that we operate and ride in or on, from snowmobiles to jet planes.

Russia, the United States and Saudi Arabia are the big producers of oil each year. Perhaps it is better to say that they are the big extractors of oil each year since the material was produced by natural processes. The countries with the largest oil reserves are Saudi Arabia with 24% of the world total reserves, followed by Russia 14%, Iraq 9%, Kuwait 9%, Venezuela 6%, Iraq 6% and United Arab Emirates 6%. The United States which uses about one third of the world's oil supply each year has only three percent of the world reserve. At the present rate of consumption the usable oil of the world will be gone by the year 2030.

The United States oil reserves are located mostly in Texas, California, Oklahoma and Louisiana. Smaller deposits are found scattered around the country.

Except for Venezuela and Mexico most of Latin America was believed to be devoid of oil. However, a large pool was discovered in Columbia. Perhaps, our estimates of world oil reserves is inaccurate. Large countries with very little known oil reserves include India, Germany, France, Pakistan, Australia and Thailand.

When it looked like the United States was going to lose its international sources of cheap oil the government began exploring the possibility of exploiting its large deposits of oil shale found in Colorado, Wyoming and Utah. This is a fine grained sedimentary rock impregnated with oil. When crushed and heated the rock gives off an oil material known as kerogen. This oil can be refined to produce gasoline and other products associated with oil. If necessary this source of oil will last us for at least thirty years. Mining and processing oil shale is obviously detrimental to the environment.

There are also deposits of tar and oil sands around the world. One of the largest deposits of oil sand is found in western Canada near the Athabaska River. Canadians are busy extracting and experimenting with these deposits. By year 2010, Canada expects its oil sands to produce half of its domestic oil supply.

NATURAL GAS

Natural gas is found in association with coal and oil deposits. It is the ideal fuel since it burns completely and is easy to transport. It is most used in industry, especially the glass industry and in home heating and cooking. It, however, is poisonous when inhaled in quantity and explosive when ignited.

At the present rate of consumption world natural gas supplies should last about forty years. The countries with the biggest reserves include Russia 25%, Uzbekistan 15 %, Iran 14%, Qatar 5% and United Arab Emirates 4%. The United States has slightly less than three percent of the world reserve.

Most of the Russian supply of natural gas is piped west to countries of Europe. Even though Russia has enormous gas resources compared to the rest of the world much of it is in cold and remote areas that make exploitation difficult.

NUCLEAR ENERGY

Nuclear power comes from the chain reaction of radioactive uranium. When an uranium 235 atom is struck by a neutron given off by another uranium 235 nuclei the uranium is split into fragments. As the reaction continues other atoms are split. This is nuclear fission and it produces heat.

About ninety seven percent of uranium ore contains uranium 238 which is stable. Less than one percent of uranium ore contains uranium 235 which is radioactive. In order to make nuclear fuel the U-235 is concentrated (enrichment). This enriched fuel is inserted into steel tubes or fuel rods. These half inch rods are about twelve feet long. They are bundled together according to the strength of fuel desired, usually in bundles of 100 to 300 rods.

These fuel rods are lowered into the reactor core where the nuclear fission takes place. The intensity of the chain reaction of the fuel rods is controlled by neutron absorbing control rods. These are made of cadmium or boron steel. The control rods of many European reactors are made of carbon.

The control rods are raised or lowered into the reactor to control the rate of fission. By lowering the control rods completely into the reactor, fission can be completely shut down or neutralized.

13-3 Nuclear reactor cooling towers on Three Mile Island near Harrisburg, Pennsylvania. On March 29, 1979, one of two reactors lost its coolant water. This near disaster caused a halt to America's planned nuclear reactor construction. Since then, no new facilities have come on line.

The energy from the fisson of the fuel in the rods heats confined water to more than the boiling point. This water is circulated past other water in separate pipes which is heated to boiling and produces steam. This steam is used to turn turbines and produce electricity.

The reactor vessel is housed in a containment building. If the reactor core is on the way to becoming overheated the containment building can be flooded with cold water to cool down the core.

Nuclear power accounts for eighteen percent of the electricity produced in the United States. Nuclear power is environmentally safe, that is, it doesn't produce acid rain or gases detrimental to the ozone layer. Nuclear power reduces our dependence on foreign oil. This will be more important in the future as our oil reserves

become depleted. Despite the negative publicity, nuclear power produces low radiation exposure to the general public.

On the downside, nuclear power produces highly radioactive waste which must be put in steel barrels and buried in caves or underground. This will remain radioactive for thousands of years and will be a burden to our grandchildren and their grandchildren will have to deal with it. As yet, there is no permanent waste disposal site in operation and the waste is being stored temporarily at the power plants.

Nuclear mishaps at Three Mile Island in Pennsylvania and Chornobyl in the Ukraine (Chernobyl in Russian) have made the public uneasy. At Three Mile Island on March 28, 1979 the nuclear core started to melt down and was exposed to air. A radioactive hydrogen bubble developed which was finally brought under control after a week of experimentation.

The Chornobyl accident occurred on April 26, 1987. In the accident the top blew out of the containment building and sent radioactive contamination to most countries of eastern Europe. This made much of the crops and livestock in the contaminated area unusable.

There is no doubt that radiation increases the incidence of cancer, especially leukemia, bone cancer, lung cancer and skin cancer. Even low levels of exposure can result in an increase in birth defects. Further study needs to document the effects of extremely low levels of radiation over a long period of time, perhaps twenty to forty years.

Nuclear power plants are expensive to build and their waste products are expensive to handle and store. The idea behind nuclear power is enticing. A load of enriched uranium the size of a large desk will produce the same amount of electricty as three and half million tons of coal and there are no ashes to handle.

13-4 Nuclear cooling towers.

LEADING COUNTRIES AND NUMBER OF NUCLEAR ENERGY UNITS (1995)

World total	430	Canada	22
United States	109	Germany	21
France	57	Ukraine	15
Japan	48	Sweden	12
United Kingdom	35	Spain	9
Russia	29		

SCHEMES FOR ALTERNATE ENERGY SOURCES

Ancient people worshipped the sun and why not, when it comes down to it, all energy and all life depends on the sun. The sun is responsible for the hydrologic cycle which gives us running streams, the wind, the tides and plant growth. It is obvious that we are too dependent on fossil fuels for our supplies of energy. The following is a brief discussion of alternate possibilities for energy which will reduce our dependency on fossil fuels.

Solar Energy: We can heat our houses by having large windows and letting the sun's rays come through. This is a simple passive solar system of energy. We can also let the sun shine on water heaters and circulate the hot water to bathe in. The sun will heat stones during the day and they will radiate heat at night to keep us warm. There are many adaptations of passive solar energy and one has only to think about them awhile to see that there is much potential there.

Active solar systems utilize solar collectors hooked up to solar cells. The most common solar cells used today are found in hand-held calculators. Industrialized countries around the world are busily trying to perfect the solar cell that will provide electricity cheaply. Leaders in this research are the scientists of Japan, Italy and Germany.

13-5 A turbo-generator is lowered into place at the electric generator station of the Grand Coulee Dam in Washington. There are no longer any large sites for hydroelectric power available in the United States.

Solar electric cells could provide much of our electricity of the future. Perhaps these can be used in the high sun months of summer and the conventional power systems used in winter thus conserving our fossil fuels.

Solar cells are easy to install, they take little maintentance and once installed will last for at least thirty years. Although solar cells are mostly silicon, which is an abundant mineral, they contain small amounts of cadmium or gallium which are rare. At present the cost of solar electricty is almost twice that of coal produced electricty. In the future the cost should become more competitive.

Solar powered cars might be the wave of the future. Each year, engineers develop new solar powered cars and race them somewhere in the world. The winner of a race in Australia moved his car more than two thousand miles at an average speed of forty miles per hour.

Wind Power: Windmills have been used for centuries to grind grain and pump water. Today the wind can be used to generate electricity. Investigation into wind power became more intense in the 1970's and by 1987 there were almost 14,000 wind generators in California which produced enough electricty for a million people. By the turn of the century, California hopes to provide ten percent of its electricty by wind power.

Water of Sea and Stream: There are many experimental electric generators hooked up to

99

various coasts with exceptionally high tides. Basically as the tide comes in, it turns a generator as it pours through a narrow inlet. As it exits the shore the generator is reversed and the outflow again turns it in the desired direction.

Tide electricity facilities are expensive to build. And, it is possible that they will be subjected to severe storms. The few generators that exist have been very successful and this holds some promise for the future.

Experiments with wave generation of electricity have proved that it can be done. Several generating stations in France which were expensive installations are presently generating electricty. This form of power will have to be considered experimental and presently not feasible.

Hydropower, that is, the movement of water in streams has been used to grind grain, saw timber, power textile mills and move many types of other machines. Today we have great hydropower installations around the world.

Hydropower is inexpensive and it is pollution free. Once built the installation takes few workers to run it. The problems though are many. They are expensive to build and those in operation are presently having their water reservoirs filled with sediment. In the construction of these, good farmland and wildlife habitat are usually buried.

The Earth's Storehouse of Heat: With the invention of the heat pump it has been possible to extract heat from the air and water. The heat pump contains a gas such as ammonia which condenses and evaporates at reasonable temperatures. Even what we might consider to be cool air at thirty five degrees Fahrenheit has much heat in it. This air is brought into the heat pump, heat is extracted from it and the air is sent back to the outside.

The same is true for ground water. Water in the earth is heated by the earth's heat. This water can be pumped into a heat extractor pump and the heat removed and the water then sent back down into the earth to be reheated.

Heat can also be removed from ocean water under the same conditions. It is possible that we can have heat extractors riding on the ocean and have the heat or electricity created by the heat sent to shore.

The problem with heat pumps is that they take electricity to operate. If they are used to create electricity then there is no gain in energy. It will take as much energy to run the system as it creates.

Geothermal energy has proven to be more rewarding. Enormous amounts of heat is stored deep underground. This can be the result of small amounts of radioactivity or where geological activity is taking place such as along fault zones. These hot rock zones are capable of boiling water and when this water comes to the surface it shoots out forming geysers or runs out creating hot springs and streams.

There is a lot of subsurface heat in volcanic areas. Many countries such as Japan and Italy have tapped into this heat source.

Besides the obvious hot zones such as volcanism and earthquake areas, geologists have identified geothermal convection zones where the natural heat of the earth migrates in a predictable convection pattern.

The capital city of Iceland, Reykjavik, has used earth's thermal heat for years. The steam from an active volcano is used to generate electricty and the steam is used directly to heat houses in the city. Steam heat is also used in Iceland to heat greenhouses which supplies the city with out-of-season vegetables.

Volcanic steam is also used to generate electricty in New Zealand, Russia, the Philippines, Italy, Mexico, Japan and the United States.

In the United States geothermal electricty is produced in California, Montana, Wyoming and North Dakota. California has

13-6 Old Faithful Geyser spews forth at Yellowstone National Park. Geysers, fault lines and volcanoes indicate thermal areas underground which can be exploited for their energy.

the biggest potential for producing large amounts of geothermal electricty. The generating plants are cheaper to build than conventional coal-fired or nuclear systems since there is no need for a source of fuel. By the year 2020, California should be generating one fourth of its electricty with geothermal energy.

Wood and Biomass Potential: Half of the world's population depends upon wood for its main source of cooking and heating fuel. Most of this takes place in the poorer Third World. But even in countries such as the United States, Sweden, Norway, Finland and Canada more than ten percent of home heating is carried on with wood.

Unfortunately in Third World countries wood resources are being depleted faster than they are grown. Most trees are gone from the fringe areas of the deserts and other low rainfall regions. In areas such as the

plateaus of Latin America, Himalayas and on many islands such as Haiti the wood resources are almost gone.

The depletion of wood resources creates enormous problems for the environment. These include desertification, erosion, flooding and habitat destruction.

The Third World, and indeed every other world, must be taught the philosophy of sustained yield and conservation. Efficient cooking and heating stoves have been designed and these should be made available to villagers who now cook over open fires.

Everyone must learn to substitute cheap energy sources for those more expensive. Wind power can be used instead of electricity in many areas of the world to pump water and grind grain.

Biomass refers to any vegetable or animal matter. Biomass has not really been considered as an alternate source of energy for the world. We can create methane gas from decaying vegetation and manure. The gas can be used to heat buildings and run electric generators. This is being done in rural India where there is an abundance of manure. However, the manure used in this manner is taken from the fields which desperately needs the fertilizer.

Ethanol, a gasoline type product, is being made from the distillation of grain and sugar cane. Ethanol can be mixed with gasoline to create a product called gasohol which is effective in running conventional motor vehicles. Brazil which has an abundance of sugar cane runs about thirty percent of its vehicles on ethanol. In the next twenty years it expects to run all of its vehicles on pure alcohol made from sugar cane. However, there have recently been big cutbacks in this program.

Unfortunately, the creation of ethanol takes as much energy to produce as it creates. We are merely converting one form of energy to another and there is no gain in the transfer. If solar or wind power is used to operate the distillation apparatus then it is possible to gain energy in the creation of alcohol and ethanol.

CONSERVING OUR ENERGY RESOURCES

During the Energy Crunch of the 1960's and 1970's the United States gave much attention to the problem of conserving our energy resources and finding alternative energy. Once gasoline became inexpensive the country forgot about its long range plans and returned to a live-for-the-moment philosophy.

Since the automobile takes most of our energy resources it seems logical to begin there. We can enforce car pooling, riding on public transportation, and develop vehicles that double the present miles per gallon of gasoline.

Houses can be made energy efficient by insulation and using more energy efficient appliances and heating systems. Simple changes such as efficient light bulbs and shower heads can make a tremendous difference in the total energy bill.

We can change our philosophy as to what are necessities and what are luxuries. For instance, the United States uses more energy to run its air conditioners than the entire energy use of the country of China. The extra lighting in the city of Las Vegas, Nevada uses more electricity than a conventional city of five million people.

By lowering the room thermostat setting from 72 to 68 degrees there will be a saving of fifteen percent on the electric bill over the course of a winter. Savings can also be made by checking the house for drafts and covering these areas with caulking or weather stripping. Turning down the setting of water heaters to 120 degrees is also a cost cutting measure.

Electric Cars

Cars cause more air pollution than any other source. The two most promising energy sources for cars of the future are electricity from batteries and the use of hydrogen. Most states are moving to a standard of auto emissions that will make driving with gasoline an expensive enterprise.

Electric cars give off no emissions. They store electricity in batteries and use it to drive electric motors. Electric cars do not contribute to urban smog or greenhouse warming, at least not directly.

At the present time, most electricity in the United States is produced by burning coal. Since these coal power plants are in rural areas the net effect will be to reduce urban smog.

However, the power plants which burn fossil fuels are twice as efficient as vehicles which burn gasoline. So for each thousand miles traveled the net effect is less pollution.

Batteries are not yet available that will make electric cars feasible. The experimental batteries have a high cost of production and use toxic materials in their construction.

102

14 HARMFUL SUBSTANCES

From 1980 to 1995 more than 400,000 deaths a year in the United States were attributed to the greatest environmental hazard to human life. What was the hazard? It was the use of tobacco. In that same time period, automobile accidents killed about 45,000 a year and hard drugs 30,000. A twenty year old man or woman in good health who uses tobacco cannot imagine that thirty years later they might be dying from some activity that did not seem to be harmful at the time.

A hazard is any substance that can cause disease, injury or environmental damage. Hazards are measured by statistical analysis and computer models tell us the probability of the hazard affecting our lives.

The effects of the hazard depends upon the type of hazard, perhaps a chemical in the air, how long the time of exposure, the health and age of the individual exposed and how well parts of the body respond to eliminating the hazard. If the effects are immediate it is labeled acute and if it is a long lasting effect due to exposure over a long period of time it is a chronic effect.

Cultural hazards are those produced by our living and working conditions and by our activities such as drinking alcoholic beverages. This would also include our attitudes toward driving and unsafe sexual activities. Pollution is usually the result of cultural activities.

Physical hazards include weather phenomena such as tornadoes and earthquakes. These would also include natural fires and noise. Mountain climbing is a cultural activity that includes physical hazards.

HAZARDOUS ENVIRONMENTAL SUBSTANCES

There are thousands of chemicals and other substances in the environment that can be dangerous to human health. We need not worry about most of them since they exist in amounts too small to be a threat to humans. However, some of them exist in large quantities and in these quantities can be hazardous. Some others, even in small amounts can be deadly. A few of these are listed below.

Carbon Monoxide

When we breathe in carbon monoxide, it combines readily with our blood. It combines more than 200 times faster with hemoglobin than does oxygen. Breathing in even a small amount of carbon monoxide for a full workday decreases oxygen in the body equivalent to a loss of one pint of blood.

Carbon monoxide is colorless and odorless. When we are in a lot of traffic, carbon monoxide build-up can be a serious threat to our ability to reason.

People with heart disease, asthma and lung disorders are especially vulnerable to carbon monoxide poisoning. Carbon monoxide coupled with high altitude and high humidity are double dangerous.

Cigaret smoke contains 300 parts per million of carbon dioxide. This reduces hemoglobin oxygen in the non-smoker as well as the smoker. Cigaret smoking along with heavy traffic and industrial pollution is a serious threat to life.

Lead

Lead poisoning causes mental retardation in children. Adults have the ability to pass off excess lead in their urine. However, in adults, lead coupled with high blood pressure can be dangerous.

High levels of lead in humans was attributed to leaded gasoline and the fumes resulting from its combustion. It was also found that the gaseous lead settled on plants and that such things as garden vegetables grown in high traffic areas had high amounts of lead on them. This lead on fruits and vegetables is easily removed by washing.

Peeling paint in rural areas was responsible for several documented cases of lead in groundwater supplies. Peeling paint in older houses is believed to be the source of excess lead in school children. Most school districts now check for lead in children. Lead found in drinking water is now the most serious threat from this substance. This comes from lead solder found in most waterpipes.

Airborne lead can be the result of burning slick magazines. The paints and dyes used in the magazines have other heavy metals besides lead.

The Environmental Protection Agency has banned the use of leaded gasoline but it is still manufactured and used in such things as chain saws and lawn mowers. We should suspect any anti-knock additive to gasoline. These substitutes for lead may be just as damaging to the environment and human health. Any gasoline gives off a plethora of undesirable gases when burned.

Asbestos

Asbestos is a fibrous mineral heavily mined in Canada, Russia and South Africa, It is known as mineral wool and has been used in fire prevention and heat retainment structures. Major uses are in furnaces, face masks, hot pipes, oil lamp wicks, iron board pads, brake linings, plasterboard and plaster.

As asbestos ages, small flakes get into the air and into the lungs. These act as tiny knives that cut the lungs. The lungs respond by growing scar tissue around the cuts. These appear as red-yellow growths in the lungs and reduces lung breathing capacity. The disease is called asbestosis.

Asbestos lungs are further aggravated by cigarette smoking. Lung cancer deaths are extremely high among asbestos workers that smoked.

There is a national campaign to remove asbestos from all schools. Older schools have asbestos in flooring material, plaster and ceiling tile and covering for water and furnace pipes. However, research indicates that there has been no harmful effects from asbestos in these school construction items as long as it remains undisturbed. Perhaps the billions of dollars spent on removing asbestos was an unnecessary expense.

Mercury

Mercury is a metal found in liquid form at normal temperatures. Its deadly effects were recognized in ancient times and it was a common substance used in murders and suicide.

About five thousand tons of mercury is put into the environment by mining and industrial uses of the mercury ore, cinnabar (HgS) and the burning of coal.

Inorganic mercury and its vapors do not pass through cell tissue easily. It damages liver, intestines and kidneys. Organic mercury (methyl mercury) passes easily through cell tissue and is readily absorbed in the food chain. When humans eat fish contaminated with mercury, then mercury poisoning results. It eventually results in irreversible nerve and brain damage. If the intake of mercury ceases before a critical point is reached then recovery will result.

In the Japanese town of Minamata, severe mercury poisoning resulted when its citizens ate contaminated tuna and swordfish. The poisoning was first recognized when birds fell from the air and were eaten by cats. The affliction was called the "disease of the dancing cats".

The illness now known as Minamata Disease first attacked the families of fishermen. Its first symptoms were fatigue, irritability, headaches, numbness in body parts and subtle hearing loss. Eventually vision became blurred. Babies were born with congenital defects. Before the disease was officially identified 43 people had died and 112 were severely disabled.

Other heavy metals which are hazardous to human health include arsenic, bismuth, cadmium, chromium, copper, gold, lead, nickel, platinum, selenium, silver, thallium and vanadium. Each of these has important uses in our modern society. They escape into the

14-1 A pollution warning sign posted at a shore entrance to Puget Sound, Washington. Since they are almost immobile, shellfish are one of the first sea creatures to become contaminated.

environment during mining, manufacturing and final disposal. Less than twenty years ago a common method of disposal of heavy metal wastes was to dump them into lakes, streams and the ocean. The metals are still there today and clean-up of these is almost impossible.

Dioxin

There are about 80 known dioxin compounds that are distinguished from each other by the chemical arrangement of the chlorine atoms in a molecule. Dioxins contain hydrogen, oxygen, carbon and chlorine. The most deadly of the dioxin molecules is TCDD.

Dioxin is a by-product of chemical reactions in the manufacturing process and also the result of smokestack burning at low temperatures. It is the dioxin in pesticides, especially Agent Orange, which is the lethal ingredient.

Exposure to dioxin produces a condition known as chloracne (chlorine-acne) which may be accompanied by loss of appetite and weight as well as liver disorders and nerve damage. Exposure to even small amounts of TCDD will result in eventual cancer.

Once formed, dioxin persists in the environment and there is no feasible way of getting rid of it. In 1983, the town of Times Beach, Missouri was contaminated with dioxin from oil sprayed on its gravel roads to alleviate a dust problem. The federal government purchased the entire town and evacuated its 2400 residents. There are probably more than a thousand sites in the United States contaminated with dioxin as well as many bodies of water, such as the Great Lakes.

Pesticides

Ever since humans arrived on earth they have been bothered by pests in various forms. These have given humans competition for food, threatened human health and some have simply made life miserable.

To control the pests, various ways of killing or abating their numbers have been devised. The first pesticides were various forms of sulfur, lead, arsenic and mercury. When the New World was invaded by Europeans, they adopted nicotine and other plant derivations such as curare into their pesticide arsenal.

The recent expansion of modern pesticides can be traced to World War II when DDT (Dichlorodiphenytrichloroethane) was invented. It killed disease spreading and plant eating insects by the billions. Cows were sprayed with it to eliminate ticks and since it persisted on the animal, it killed flies that landed on them.

About twenty years after the invention of DDT, it was discovered that it caused a considerable amount of environmental damage. DDT collected in fatty tissue of humans as well as animals. Birth defects were connected to DDT. If a human ate a fish containing DDT, the chemical became part of the human. DDT was especially disastrous to wild birds, such as the Bald Eagle, which feed on fish which feed on water organisms. Eventually DDT was banned from use in the United States. However, it is still used in many Lesser Developed Countries.

Today, there are about 60,000 different chemical pesticides on the market. These are sold mostly to kill insects, weeds, rodents, fungi, mites and ticks. We associate pesticides with farming but homeowners used about five times more pesticides per acre than farmers. One fifth of our pesticides is used on lawns, golf course, parks, gardens and cemeteries. More than a billion and a half dollars a year is spent on lawn care in the United States.

Pesticides include insecticides, rodenticides, herbicides and fungicides. Each has its own target specialty. Each has its advantages and disadvantages.

Insecticides are mostly phosphate, carbonate and chlorinated hydrocarbon compounds which includes pyrethroids, heptachlor, toxaphene, chlordane, kepone and mirex. Many of these stay in the environment for at least twelve years. They function by damaging the insect nervous system. These insecticide chemicals are slowly being replaced by others which have a shorter persistence in the environment.

Phosphate insecticides have a persistence measured in weeks but they are particularly harmful to humans, birds and fish. Phosphates are water soluble so they are more likely to contaminate water supplies. Since phosphate insecticides only last a few weeks, farmers are more likely to use them several times over the period of one growing season. Malathion and Parathion are the most used phosphate insecticides.

Carbonate and pyrehroid pesticides are active only a few days, but extremely harmful if improperly applied.

Rodenticides are used to kill rats and mice. Most of these are sodium fluoroacetate which attack the nervous system. Other rodenticides, sold over the counter and applied in houses cause rodents to get thirsty and go outside in search of water. Once outside, they hemorrhage and die.

Herbicides are active for only a short time. In that time they are used as defoliants or to sterilize the soil. Contact herbicides kill the plant quickly. Others are taken into the plant vascular system to eventually kill it. The popular contact herbicides are triazines, atrazines and paraquat. The system absorbing chemicals are 2,4-D and 2,4,5-T. The latter, which contains an ingredient called Agent Orange, has been banned in the United States.

Herbicides which sterilize the soil kill

14-2 Spraying cacao trees in the tropics. When we import tropical products such as coffee, chocolate and bananas we also import some pesticides with them.

microorganisms essential to plant growth. Most of these also get into the vascular system of plants which kill them and eventually make the soil barren. Later this sterile area can be planted and fertilized to produce crops.

Fungicides are mostly used to protect seeds before planting. These use arsenic, lead and mercury. Humans eating the contaminated seed can develop a number of afflictions and death is common. Humans have become ill and died from eating hogs and chickens which had eaten contaminated seeds. Most treated seeds are now dyed purple or red in order to warn the user that a fungicide has been applied.

Fungicides are also used to counteract human fungi afflictions such as ringworm, athlete's foot and mildew. Fungus skin infections are extremely painful.

THE CASE FOR PESTICIDES

Pesticides are mobile, they can be applied in one area of the world and end up thousands of miles away. They are carried by air and water. The are carried in the bodies of fish and birds. They stay in water sediments indefinitely. When the sediments are dredged, the pesticides enter the environment once again.

Pesticides destroy beneficial insects as well as harmful insects. They cause resistant strains of insects to develop. If two percent of sprayed flies survive, they will unite to foster a new super breed of flies.

The biological magnification of pesticides is one of society's horrors. A fish eats the contaminated larva which ate the contaminated plant. We eat the fish. It is logical then to eat only small fish instead of lunkers since they have less contaminants. Fish stocked by hatcheries are usually free of contaminants.

However, before we condemn pesticides we must keep in mind that insects kill over a

107

million people a year and cause another 300 million people to become ill. Mosquitoes spread malaria, yellow fever and encephalitis. Ticks spread Lyme Disease and spotted fever. Fleas spread bubonic plague and typhus. Various flies spread hundreds of different diseases to both humans and animals.

Consider also that insects eat about thirty percent of the United States crop and fifty percent of the world crop each year. This is before and after harvest. When we consider this insect devastation coupled with loss to weather, birds, weeds and mammals, it is a wonder we can produce the amount of crops we do.

The ideal pesticide would be very selective and kill only its target. It should have a short life in the environment and decompose harmlessly. It should save more money than that lost to the pest and it should limit the development of genetically resistant pests. So far the ideal pesticide does not exist.

Farmers can limit the use of pesticides with crop rotation, strip cropping and developing trap crops which is a crop that takes the insect away from the desired crop.

For best environmental results we should consider Integrated Pest Management (IPM). This is a method of reducing pests while natural factors that help manage them are enhanced. The goal of IPM is to reduce the size of the pest population below the injury level rather than to eliminate the pest entirely. Perhaps the best control is picking the pest off the crop by hand or simply stepping on it.

Consider the following methods of pest control. Use proper plant selection. Choose varieties of plants that are well adapted to the climate. Some are more resistant to diseases than others.

Handpick, shake or wash off pests rather than spray them with pesticides. Use barriers such as screens or insect repellents to ward off insects. Use traps for flies, mice and beetles.

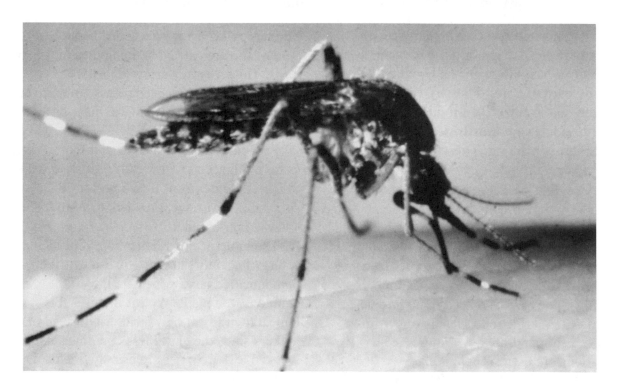

14-3 Mosquito bites cause more than 3 million illnesses a year. Mosquitoes spread many diseases including malaria, yellow fever and encephalitis. However, when we kill mosquitoes we affect the food supply of several animal species including frogs and birds.

Many newer traps contain insect sex attractants. Where possible use the sterile male technique, that is releasing sterilized male of the species to mate with receptive females, thus there are no offspring.

Put up bird houses to attract flycatchers, bluebirds and swallows. Use BT, Bacillus thuringeinsis to kill larva. This is a biodegradable bacteria which is harmless to humans. It is used to kill caterpillars on cabbage type plants.

IS YOUR LAWN WORTH THE RISK?

Lawn care chemicals are designed to fertilize lawns and kill unwanted plants, insects and fungus. The poisons used in these mixtures include herbicides such as 2,4-D, insecticides such as Dursban and fungicides such as Captan.

Long term problems associated with lawn care poisons include lowered male fertility, miscarriage, birth defects, chemical sensitivity, liver and kidney damage, heart disturbances and cancer. Immediate adverse symptoms include depression, anxiety, irritability, vomiting, dizziness, fatigue, headache, diarrhea, coughing and asthma-like attacks.

There are no laws to protect you from being poisoned by lawn care chemicals. According to Congressional records nine out of ten pesticides in use today were registered with health testing that is non-existent, incomplete or fraudulent. It is a violation of federal law to label any chemical pesticide as "safe", "harmless", or "non-toxic to humans or pets".

Most doctors are not familiar with the symptoms of chronic low-dose pesticide poisoning. This condition is most often diagnosed as allergies, asthma or the flu.

Lawns can be healthy if they are planted in a natural environment, not in a desert or some place where grasses do not exist. Leaving grass clippings on the lawn is the easiest way to handle them and it adds fertility to the soil. Leaving clippings on the lawn helps build a community of microorganisms and earthworms which help to keep the lawn healthy. Many lawn mower companies now advertise the "mulching" lawn mower which shreds the grass to small size and leaves it on the lawn.

Major Crops Treated With Pesticides

Insecticides: 1. pears 2. apples 3. citrus
4. almonds 5. grapes

Herbicides: 1. rice 2. peanuts 3. corn
4. cotton 5. cotton 6. sorghum
7. soybeans

COMMON CHEMICAL CONTAMINANTS OF DRINKING WATER (danger to)

arsenic - nervous system
benzene - genetic material
cadmium - kidneys, bladder
carbon tetrachloride - liver, kidneys, lungs
chloroform - liver, kidneys
dioxin - causes many cancers
ethylene dibromide - male sterility
lead - birth defects
mercury - nervous system
nitrates - respiratory system
PCBs - liver, kidneys, heart
trichloroethylene - nervous system, liver, kidneys, skin problems
vinyl chloride - liver, kidney, heart, stomach

Hazardous Properties
1. Flammable: catches fire easily
    solvents, gasoline
2. Toxic: poisonous
    pesticides, various cleaning fluids
3. Corrosive: causes burns
    oven and drain cleaners
4. Reactive: causes chemical reactions
    ammonia, bleaches of all kinds

15 WASTE DISPOSAL

Everything you are wearing and everything in the room with you will eventually become waste. It will all have to be thrown away or disposed in some manner.

The United States contains less than five percent of the world's population but produces one third of the world's solid waste. Our per capita solid waste amounts to 44 tons a year. This comes, not only from individual daily throw away waste, which amounts to four and a half pounds per person, but from industry and agriculture which manufacture products we use.

About eighty five percent of the United States waste is generated by mining and industry. By tonnage, most of this is mine waste which is piled around the mine site.

The second largest creator of solid waste is agriculture which produces large amounts of stems, vines, stalks, twigs, leaves and manure. Industrial solid waste is third in landfill weight. This includes scrap metal, plastics, paper and sludge. A large amount of fly ash is generated by coal fueled electric plants and municipal incinerators.

Municipalities generate 185 million tons of solid waste a year. Each individual person generates about 1600 pounds of garbage a year. Most of this ends up in landfills. Many municipalities such as Philadelphia pay over a hundred dollars a ton to use present landfills.

Broken down by producers the solid waste generation for the United States for 1995 was Mining 75%, Agriculture 13%, Industry 10% and Municipal 2%. Most of the municipal waste ends up in landfills, 73%, but incineration is increasing, 14%. Another 12% is recycled and only one percent is composted. Efforts are being made to increase recycling and composting.

Paper and cardboard make up about a third of household waste. This includes newspapers, paper towels, napkins and food packaging. Much of this could be recycled but adequate paper recycling plants are still a few years away.

Municipal solid waste by weight in the United States in 1995 included paper 41%, yard wastes 18%, food 9%, metals 9%, glass 8%, wood 3%, leather and rubber 3% and cloth one percent. Almost all of this can be recycled or composted.

We usually deal with the growing solid waste pile by burning or burying it. It would be better if we cut down on production of materials which will become solid waste in our throw-away society. Most packaging of food, tools, toys and the like products come with too much wrapping. Even though this has benefits in handling and retailing it is a waste of valuable resources.

Burning solid waste such as paper produces air pollution. Even the best designed incineration systems produce airborne toxic substances. Burning plastics may create dioxins. The waste ash of incineration is also toxic and must be disposed with care, usually in a hazardous waste dump. These waste dumps are always a threat to precious water supplies.

To help decrease the amount of solid waste generation we can give tax write-offs to those industries which consider the environment in their operations. Our present system of tax incentives to industry encourages production at the expense of the environment.

We must encourage low waste production and emphasize recycling and reusing waste products. Around eighty five percent of materials put in solid waste landfills can be reused or recycled. Eventually, however, everything, even the recycled products, ends up in a landfill.

Three fourths of our municipal solid waste ends up in sanitary landfills. These are garbage dumps where solid wastes are spread out in layers, compacted with bulldozers and then covered with plastic or clay each day. Modern

15-1 A tractor compacts trash on a sanitary landfill. About one-third of all landfill material is paper.

landfill regulations require the final filled landfill to be covered with clay or some impervious material. Many of the landfills are also lined with clay or plastic to prevent leaching into ground water supplies.

Since modern landfills are covered and compacted, the normal breakdown of materials by biologic processes is severely curtailed. Newspapers in a modern landfill are still readable after thirty years. Plastics may last up to 200 years before they break into small pieces.

Landfills with a lot of organic materials will produce methane gas. These landfills can explode or catch fire and smolder for years. In many landfills, gas venting pipes are inserted into the landfill to take off excess gas. The gas can then be collected and used to run machinery.

Solid waste not in landfills is usually incinerated. This has several advantages over

landfilling. It kills disease organisms and reduces the need for landfill space by ninety percent. However, it does not discourage the throw-away habit which causes many of the landfill problems in the first place.

Incineration may reduce landfill space use but it pollutes the atmosphere. Also, the residue of incineration contains concentrated toxics which must be put in landfills with care.

Many modern incinerators produce electricity while burning the trash. These are usually located near cities to take advantage of the large trash generating population. This is also where air pollution from burning does the greatest damage.

Also on the negative side of incineration, is the fact that recycling paper will save five times more energy than is generated by burning. Incinerators are very expensive to build. Even the most efficient of them produce small amounts of dioxins, acids and airborne heavy metals such as mercury, lead and cadmium.

Most conservationists believe we should limit solid waste at its source rather than deal with it as the end product. But, as the end product we can separate trash into recyclable and nonrecyclable materials. The recyclables can generate income for those involved in its collection.

Much of what is thrown away can be reused by someone else. It is a matter of finding that ultimate consumer. Goodwill Industries and the Salvation Army do a good job of collecting used furniture and clothing for redistribution. What used clothing collectors cannot immediately redistribute in America is usually sold by the pound to Third World importers. This greatly reduces pressure on our landfills.

Biodegradable yard wastes should be composted and used for soil improvement and fertilizer. This can also be done with slaughterhouse and food processing wastes as well as feed-lot manure. Compost can be produced at large recycling centers, bagged and sold at a profit. Households should have their own compost bins and the compost products used on flower beds, lawns and gardens.

Today, landfill space is becoming critical and recycling, incineration and composting will increase as the need to reduce landfill space gets even more critical. In order to reduce the volume of material going into landfills we need beverage container laws requiring the return of containers for recycling or refilling. Old tires, a quarter billion a year in the US, can be melted into crude oil or ground up for parking lot surfacing.

A tax could be placed on throw-away products and the money used to take care of that product's final disposal. For instance, every new automobile would come with a hundred dollar tax. The money would be put into a fund and used to dispose of the old automobile carcass when it has expired. A two cent tax on all tin can products would accomplish the same purpose.

We can move a long way in reducing solid waste by reducing packaging. One dollar in every ten spent in grocery stores is for packaging. Many products such as toys really need no packaging.

Manufacturers should be encouraged to make products which are easy to recycle or reuse. Consumers can encourage this by changing their purchasing habits.

Everything we own or use eventually ends up as a waste product. With environmental sensitivity we can limit our contribution to the waste stream. We can't put off the inevitable landfill shortage but we can slow it down for the present.

HAZARDOUS WASTE

Much of our waste products are considered hazardous. These are materials that contain substances which are toxic, carcinogenic or genetic threats. Hazardous also includes flammable and explodable materials as well as It also includes materials that break down to form dangerous substances such as heavy metals.

Each hazardous material has its own disposal problem. Usually the Environmental Protection Agency classifies the wastes into categories according to the most appropriate method of treatment and disposal.

Aqueous Liquid Wastes include those that are corrosive such as pickling baths and cyanides. Organic Liquid Wastes include halogenated solvents, oils, combustible liquids and other solvents. Solids and Sludges include paint residues, combustible solids and sludges, heavy metal sludges, electric arc furnace dusts and emission control dusts. The category **Other Wastes** include ignitable, corrosive, reactive and toxic materials.

These are industrial wastes and there are many methods devised to handle them.

However, much of this material is put into landfills rather than recycled, neutralized or reused.

Hazardous waste recovery facilities use solvent recovery techniques which separate the contaminants from solvents and thus restores solvents to their original quality or lower quality for reuse. Pyrometallurgical Recovery uses high temperatures to separate metals from materials, mostly ores. Hydrometallurgical Recovery concentrates heavy materials such as chromium and nickel by various weight separation processes. Acid Regeneration involves separation of unused acid from pickling baths. Fuel Blending creates usable products by taking used oils and solvents and blending them with fresh materials having a high BTU value.

Hazardous wastes can also be treated to neutralize their hazardous properties. Incineration is a major treatment. Wet Air Oxidation involves oxidation reactions identical to combustion but occurring in a liquid state with elevated pressure and temperatures. Advanced Thermal Destruction which uses elevated temperatures as the primary means of treatment has not yet been perfected.

Land disposal systems involve surface impoundments which holds the materials until other means of disposal can be implemented. There are about 78,000 of these in the United States and there seems to be no great rush to treat the materials.

Landfill disposal involves permanent emplacement of hazardous waste. Nobody seems to want this type of landfill in their neighborhoods and we have developed the NIMBY CONCEPT which stands for "Not in my backyard". We use the products that generates hazardous wastes but we don't seem to want to be part of the disposal of the

15-2 Trucks and hampers are put out to collect newspapers and plastics for recycling. Recycling uses less energy than starting with raw materials. Recycling is one method of saving landfill space.

15-3 Liquid chemical wastes are transported in trucks such as this. Most liquid wastes are disposed in injection wells.

wastes created by these products.

There are many federal regulations covering hazardous waste landfills. These involve prohibition of certain wastes such as those with high radioactivity, use of plastic or clay liners, leak detection leachate collection, impervious caps, ground water monitoring and perpetual maintenance.

Eventually the plastic and clay liners will begin to leak. By that time, the owners of the landfills will be out of business and there will be no responsible parties to clean up the threat and the cost of clean-up will fall back to the federal government.

Let us not get the impression that only industry puts hazardous materials into landfills. We have only to look in the mirror to see someone who uses hazardous materials and must dispose of them. For instance our hazardous materials which go into landfills include batteries, antifreeze, motor oil, rust removers, disinfectants, toilet cleaners, oven cleaners, spot removers, oil base paints, paint strippers, wood preservatives, driveway and roof tars, pesticides, flea powder, glues and deodorants. These are not necessarily hazardous unless they get into our water

supplies. Once in a landfill it is only a matter of time until they get into a water system.

LOW-LEVEL RADIOACTIVE WASTE DISPOSAL

Putting low-level radioactive wastes into hazardous waste landfills instead of the more secure radioactive waste disposal systems is a cause for much debate between environmentalists and those who produce such wastes. Low-level radioactive waste includes such things as rags, papers, protective clothing, filters, gloves which comes from making electrical energy by nuclear facilities, medical facilities and industrial and medical research. It is also created by the manufacture of smoke alarms and other warning devices.

Low level wastes do not include used fuel rods from nuclear power plants and highly radioactive waste from weapons manufacturing. These are handled by the federal government at separate waste disposal sites.

Low-level waste is classified according to the amount of radioactivity it contains. States are responsible for the disposal of low-level radioactive wastes. Disposal sites will not accept low-level wastes in the form of liquids or gases, only solids.

Each state must take steps to provide for the safe disposal of low-level wastes generated within their borders. If a state does not provide for the disposal, the state may be barred from using any of the present disposal sites operated under federal jurisdiction.

High level radioactive disposal involves plutonium which is an element that exists in trace amounts in nature but is manufactured in large amounts in nuclear reactors. Plutonium is created by bombarding atoms of uranium U 238 until they absorb a neutron and become Pu 239. The Department of Energy operates thirteen sites for storage and disposal of plutonium. These storage sites which contain about 28 tons of plutonium are aging and possibly pose a threat to their surroundings.

The plutonium storage sites are located at Hanford WA, Argonne West ID, Rocky Flats CO, Pantex TX, Los Alamos NM, Sanda NM, Lawrence Livermore CA, Lawrence Berkeley CA, New Brunswick IL, Argonne East IL, Mound OH, Oak Ridge TN and Savannah River SC. All of these are classified as temporary disposal sites, but we do not yet have an operational permanent disposal site for high-level radioactive wastes.

SUPERFUND

A fund established by federal and state governments has been created to clean up inactive hazardous waste dump sites around the United States. It was first initiated in the Comprehensive Environmental Response Compensation and Liability Act of 1980. It has since been known as Superfund.

In the first phase of the act 34,000 hazardous waste sites were identified. This included almost 18,000 sites at military bases. Today, there have been almost half a million of these sites identified and the number keeps growing as these sites, usually hidden, are located.

Unfortunately, only about twelve percent of the original 16 billion dollars allocated for clean-up has gone for actual work. The rest has been used for administration, consultants and management. The entire clean-up costs will probably come close to a trillion dollars before it is completed, if it is ever completed.

Unfortunately, many of those who have created the toxic waste sites are no longer in business and cannot be prosecuted. Also, many of them that can be prosecuted have political clout because of campaign contributions and other perks for congressmen. Clean-up has been slow and there are thousands of sites to go.

Meanwhile, people live on the fringes and around these sites. The Love Canal Site is a classic and well publicized example of the situation. Love Canal is located near Niagara Falls, New York. It was an old canal filled with hazardous wastes and covered over. A builder, William Love, sold the land to the Niagara Falls school district for one dollar. An elementary school was built on the site and residences were built near it. The area had a high incidence of birth defects, miscarriages, cancer, nerve and kidney disease. Eventually, the state closed the school and permanently relocated the 238 families who lived near the dump which they could not see.

The properties around the Superfund sites have become nightmares to the people who live near them. Most of them cannot sell or simply abandon their properties. They can only wait for the federal machinery to come to clean up the sites.

Not only do we have to eradicate these sites but we must take steps to insure that no new ones are created. Is your congressman or woman willing to cooperate in this effort?

16-1 Abbala children try out a new water pump in west central Sudan. The water system was provided by WaterAid, a charity organization based in Great Britain. WaterAid accepts donations and uses the money to improve drinking water supplies and sanitation in 14 poor countries of the world. Much of the world population in poor countries has to carry water many miles and yet the water is still a source of disease and death. Approximately, 25,000 children die every day from water related diseases. Eighty percent of sickness in the world is due to unsafe water and poor sanitation.

16 FUTURE PROSPECTS

Present trends have some implications for the future. In the United States more members of the middle class are sinking into poverty. The population of the middle class is declining, poor people are increasing and more affluent (rich) people are holding steady.

Since 1980, the standard of living for the average American has been declining at the rate of four percent per year. There were more people living below the poverty line in 1995 than in the entire history of the country. There were more people unemployed in 1995 than in the Great Depression of the 1930s. We are still the country most envied around the world but that status is slowly eroding.

Most poor countries have high population increases. This results in migration to other regions. Even newly industrialized countries have population increases beyond the carrying capacity of their lands. Our neighbors are sneaking across our borders in larger numbers and putting stress on our social agencies. In 1994, more than a thousand people a day made illegal crossing of our border with Mexico. More than a hundred thousand Haitians came to Florida in make-shift boats. Almost fifty thousand Cubans entered the country illegally. Boatloads of potential illegal Chinese immigrants floundered and were rescued on both the Atlantic and Pacific coasts. This immigration, legal and illegal, coupled with our modest fertility rate will double the United States population in fifty years.

We have roughly 260 million people in the United States and by year 2040 we could have more than 500 million. This gives us a very short period of time in which we must double our social services, our schools, our water supplies, our medical services, our food resources, our sewage systems and everything else necessary to our standard of living.

No one who considers the situation can deny that our quality of life is diminishing.

Most will agree that our population has reached, if not exceeded, the carrying capacity of the environment. This has been true with most countries of the world for many years.

What is our obligation to the rest of the world? Can we continue to accept immigrants as we have done in the past? Most countries have stopped immigration altogether and only the United States, Germany, Canada and Australia still accept other peoples in large numbers. Recently Germany has enacted legislation to halt the influx of foreigners, mostly refugees from war zones.

With no increase in productivity and a doubling of our population we will simply have to accept less out of life. We can look forward to energy shortages, exhausted land, scarce water and a radical change in our diets. Our lands are already at the limit of production and crop yield increases are not going to keep up with the population growth. We will no longer have the luxury of exporting food.

The basis for our farm productivity is petroleum. We will run out of domestic petroleum supplies in twenty years and foreign sources will most likely hang on to their limited supplies. We are losing farm acres to urbanization at the rate of about 2 million acres a year. Most "thinking" countries of the world have limited the development on arable land. The United States mentality seems to think that it is the individual's right in a free society to do what one wants with private property.

Today, the average American spends about fifteen percent of income on food. In Europe and Japan the figure is thirty percent and in Lesser Developed Countries the cost runs from fifty to a hundred percent of one's income.

The hope for our future depends on legislation and regulation enacted by the United States Congress. Eventually they will be forced to recognize the desperate needs of our future and we can only hope sensible legislation which limits the profit motive as a consideration is enacted.

We must limit our population growth and wasteful use of our resources. We must treasure our water, air and soil. We must conserve, practice sustained yield and recycle.

At the beginning of 1995 there were over a hundred wars in progress. Most of these were not reported in the American press. We heard about Afghanistan, Bosnia, Chechenia, Tajikistan, Rwanda and Somalia. We heard very little about Mexico, Peru, Ecuador, Sri Lanka, Cambodia, the Philippines and Indonesia where intense fighting was carried on.

Most of these wars were over resources and a major resource was water. In this country, skirmishes are shaping up over resources of land and water. The burgeoning population centers of Southern California have already exceeded the carrying capacity of the land. Groups of citizens living in Northern California have organized to break-away from the south. How far these ideas will go depends largely on stress factors.

Los Angeles already transports most of its incoming water over three hundred miles. It uses about eight billion gallons of fresh clean water a day. Its population will double in about fifteen years. Where will it get the extra eight billion gallons of water EACH DAY.

The international community has organized meetings to discuss the implications of population, food, refugees, health and resources. Not much has been accomplished in these meetings and most countries favored their own agendas. However, what has been accomplished is the understanding that there are problems that have to be solved and most of these have to be solved on the international level.

16-2 Construction of a highway and storm drainage systems. We are losing farmland at an accelerated rate as we demand more highways and people move away from their place of employment. The move to the suburbs has caused environmental damage and increased the need for gasoline.

THE EARTH SUMMIT - Brazil 1992

The most acclaimed international meeting the world has ever seen was held in Rio de Janeiro, Brazil in June of 1992. It was the United Nations Earth Summit on the environment which hosted delegates from 178 nations including 116 heads of state.

The world expected the United States to lead the way into an environmental awareness that would have far reaching effects well into the 21st century. Instead, the United States, under the leadership of President George Bush, had a negative impact on the proceedings.

The United States insisted that carbon dioxide emission standards be eliminated from the wording of the global warming treaty. At the time of the treaty the United States with 5% of the world's people produced 23% of the world's industrial carbon dioxide.

The United States position was that the wording of the "greenhouse gas" emission treaty was too strict in its first draft and pushed for a useless high-sounding document which eventually let any nation oversee its own emissions. President Bush said his "obligation is to protect American jobs as well as the environment".

A biodiversity treaty was completely opposed by the United States and President Bush refused to sign the final draft. The treaty set aside important habitat areas in order to save and preserve diverse species. President Bush said that it would require additional U.S. aid to poor countries and would harm America's biotechnology industry.

The message from the developing countries was that they cannot afford to preserve their natural resources such as rainforests until their economies are improved by foreign aid. Without foreign aid they are forced to proceed with resource exploitation for their own economic survival.

Japan paved the way to the future when its Prime Minister Kiichi Miyazawa pledged $7.7 billion in environmental aid to developing nations. He stated that Japan would also eliminate the use of all CFCs in three years and reduce its carbon dioxide emissions to 1990 levels by the year 2000. Japan emerged as the environmental leader of the world.

It may be noted that at the time of the Summit, Japan fishing fleets still hunted whales, businesses still traded in endangered species and Japanese lumber imports were responsible for destruction of large tracts of tropical and temperate forests.

Basically, the main tenets of the Rio meeting were vague and the spirit of the meeting was its strong point. In the brief ten days, the world focused on the environment and perhaps in the future, all countries will be sensitive to the issues outlined at the meeting.

INTERNATIONAL CONFERENCE ON POPULATION AND DEVELOPMENT - 1994

Cairo, Egypt was the meeting site for the International Conference on Population and Development sponsored by the United Nations. It was assumed by the sponsors that cooperation in limiting population and increasing opportunities for poor countries would be the agenda. However, differences in culture became evident and opinions on how to improve the lot of most of the world differed.

Although the main topic was population it was really about women's rights. The original draft proposals called for a full range of reproductive and health-care services, including contraceptives and sex education for women. The organizers believed that the equality of women was the cornerstone of any population program.

The premise seemed simple enough, "what happens to a woman should be her decision". This might have been fine for most western cultures in highly developed nations but applied to other cultures it was an explosive issue.

Some Muslim clerics, from countries where women are hidden by veils and where the Koran's teachings are the law of the land, were outraged at the idea of equality for women. The agenda was an attack on their culture.

Giving the Islamic protests extra support was the Vatican led by Pope John Paul II. He accused the United Nations of trying to establish a worldwide right to abortion and demeaning the importance of the family. Catholic priests attacked the draft program for allegedly encouraging homosexuality and adolescent sex.

The American delegation was led by Vice President Albert Gore who is recognized around the world as a concerned environmentalist. He and his staff were convinced that population limitation is the world's central issue.

The American's pointed to Thailand as an example. Thirty years ago it was a poverty stricken country. Its government began to stress the importance of women's health and education. Female literacy increased to 90 percent. The average number of babies born to each woman decreased from six in 1968 to 2.1 in 1994.

Many interesting statistics were presented at the meeting. For instance, of the 960 million illiterate adults in the world, two thirds are women. Of the 130 million children denied elementary education 90 million are girls. Women are legally beaten almost everywhere.

Food per capita is falling around the world and the population continues to increase. Raising the status of women seems to be a way to counteract the dilemma. It is a tragedy that in many areas of the world women are treated as property rather than as an integral part of humanity.

In most areas of the world there are more people than the environment can support. This leads to poverty which leads to destruction of the environment. Each region has a carrying capacity and when this capacity is exceeded, extreme measures must be implemented in order for the population to survive. Food and other resources must be imported or some of the population must move out. If this cannot be accomplished, the usual result is war.

Many environmentalists believe the population of the United States has reached its carrying capacity and we are already importing many resources to compensate for the excess population. For more and more Americans, the standard of living continues to diminish. Today, there are more Americans living below the poverty level than in the entire history of the country. Despite this statistic, we are still better off than most of the world.

We became the world leader through exploitation of our natural resources, our soils, water and forests. Today, these resources are at a critical stage and we must conserve them, recycle them and practice sustainable use. Most of all - we must change our lifestyles.

pH

pH is a number value that indicates the acid or base (alkaline) nature of a substance on a scale form 0 to 14 with 7 neutral. Values above 7 are basic and values below 7 are acid in nature. Some values for commons substances are listed below.

14 lye
13 oven cleaner
12 hair remover
11 ammonia
10 Milk of Magnesia
 9 baking soda
 8 shampoo
 7 neutral, pure water
 6 urine, saliva
 5.4 environmental damage
       threshold
 5 shaving lotions
 4 tomatoes, grapes
 3 vinegar, orange juice
 2 stomach acid
 1 battery acid

NATIONAL PARK VISITORS 1992
(rounded in millions of admissions)

Smokey Mountains	8.2
Grand Canyon	3.8
Yosemite	3.2
Yellowstone	2.9
Olympic	2.8
Rocky Mountain	2.7
Acadia	2.4
Zion	2.1
Glacier	2.0
Mammoth Cave	1.9

Some worthy nongovernmental organizations

Sierra Club
408 C St. NE
Washington DC 20002

The Wilderness Society
900 17th St. NW
Washington DC 20006

National Wildlife Federation
1400 16th St NW
Washington DC 20036

For more information on rangelands, wetlands and National Parks write to:
  Bureau of Land Management,
  National Wildlife Refuge System,
  Fish and Wildlife Service,
  National Park Service
      at the
Department of the Interior
18th and C Streets NW
Washington DC 20240

For more information on farmlands, forests, soils and natural resources write to:
  Natural Resource Conservation Service
    (formerly Soil Conservation Service)
  Forest Service
write to:
Department of Agriculture
14th Street and Jefferson Dr. SW
Washington DC 20250

Occupational Safety and Health Administration
200 Constitution Ave NW
Washington DC 20210

Environmental Protection Agency
401 M Street SW
Washington DC 20460

Index to Definitions and Terms

HIGHEST OCCUPATIONAL CANCER RISKS

1. asbestos
2. vinyl chloride
3. benzene
4. arsenic
5. chromium
6. nickel
7. cadmium
8. carbon tetrachloride
9. formeldahyde
10. solvents

Regulating Agencies

Environmental Protection Agency
  pesticides, disinfectants, bleaches

Food and Drug Administration
  foods, medicines, cosmetics

Consumer Product Safety Commission
  cleaners, wood finishes, glues

SOME DISEASES FROM POLLUTED WATER

Amoebic Dysentery
Bacterial Dysentery
Cholera
Enteritis
Typhoid
Hepatitis A
Polio
Shistosis

ENVIRONMENTAL IMPACTS OF AGRICULTURE

loss of soil fertility and soil erosion
waterlogging and salinization
extinction of wildlife to clear lands for planting
air pollution from fossil fuels in mechanization
air and water pollution from use of pesticides
depletion of aquifers by excessive irrigation

SUGGESTED ESSAY QUESTIONS

1. Perhaps the greatest cause of air pollution is the construction running, and maintenance of the automobile. Do you believe that automobiles should be banned. Why or why not? What alternatives do we have to each family having its own car?

2. Generally a river will flush out its pollution. Under what conditions would a river fail to do this?

3. Since we are all partners in the generation of hazardous wastes, how would you handle the disposal of such wastes?

4. Discuss the advantages and disadvantages of living in a large city.

5. Is sending food to famine areas such as those regularly found in Africa harmful or helpful? Are there any conditions you would attach to sending such aid?

6. There are no more trees left in Haiti. How would your life-style change if wood products were no longer available or became much more expensive?

7. Keep a list of materials you throw away, dispose of, get rid of for a week - estimate its weight. What percentage of those materials could be recycled, reused, or burned as a source of energy (heat)?

8. Coal fired power plants produce more than half of this country's electricity. What action can we take to reduce our consumption of electricity, thereby avoiding 10,000 extra deaths a year? Are you willing to sacrifice TV, clothes dryers, washers, hot water, pollution caused by coal fired power plants?

9. In your opinion - is the world overpopulated? Is the United States overpopulated? Defend your position.

10. Should the United States sharply curtail legal immigration? Defend your position.

FOR FURTHER DISCUSSION
SOME ENVIRONMENTAL MYTHS (Perhaps)

1. Reusable diapers are better for the environment than disposable diapers.

    Counter argument: Reusable diapers are less sanitary. They take fuel to pick-up and deliver. They use huge volumes of fresh water to get them clean. They require detergents which in themselves are a disposal problem.

2. The Soda Pop Dilemma. Aluminum containers are the best since they are recycled easiest. Glass bottles are good since they can be reused. Plastic is bad since they last 200 years in landfills and can't be reused.

    Counter argument: Plastics are lighter and easier to transport than aluminum and glass, therefore, there is a saving on energy use. Modern hard plastic bottles can be recycled and made into other products such as planks, paving and fencing. Recycling plastic takes less energy than recycling glass or aluminum.

3. Food distribution in bulk is better than packaging since most of our packaging material ends up in landfills.

    Counter argument: When the bulk material is sold it is usually put into some sort of container. Prepackaging is sanitary, packs neatly and ships well. Bulk containers are large and unwieldy. Most packaged food is free of excess material such as bones and skin, husks and peelings. Packaging keeps such things as crackers fresh months longer than when they are in bulk, therefore there is less food wasted.

4. Non biodegradable products are bad.

5. Recycling is good for the environment.

6. Electric from nuclear energy is worse for the environment than electricity from burning coal.

7. Natural fertilizers are better than commercial chemical fertilizers.

8. Commercial insecticides do more harm than good.

9. Using a bicycle to get to work is better than using an automobile.

10. Building industrial plants in a rural area is better than locating them in a city.

1

RESOURCE TERMS

A. Briefly define the following terms:

    1. **natural resource-**

    2. **conservation-**

    3. **environment-**

    4. **habitat-**

    5. **ecosystem-**

    6. **ecological niche-**

    7. **sustained yield-**

    8. **aquatic-**

    9. **inorganic-**

    10. **recycling-**

B. Define nonrenewable resource:

1. List two nonrenewable resources and the way humans use them.

2. How can we postpone the day when the world runs out of nonrenewable resources?

C. Define renewable resource.

1. List two renewable resources and the way humans use them.

2. Is it possible for us to run out of renewable resources?
   Explain your answer.

2

THE ATMOSPHERE

A. 1. On the bar below - make a graph showing the major gases of clean, dry
air near sea level. Label each gas and give its percentage.

   2. Which gas commonly found in the atmosphere has the most variation
day to day and place to place?

```
 _____
|                                                    |
|                                                    |
|    I     I     I     I     I     I     I     I    I |
|_____|
```

B. What are the chemical designations (formulas) for the following compounds?

      1. sulfur dioxide_____   4. methane_____

      2. hydrogen sulfide_____   5. nitrogen dioxide_____

      3. carbon monoxide_____   6. sulfuric acid_____

C. What is the major source of the following atmospheric pollutants?

      1. **carbon monoxide-**_____

      2. **sulfur oxides-**_____

      3. **nitrogen oxides-**_____

      4. **particulate matter-**_____

      5. **fluorocarbons-**_____

D. List three sources of natural air pollutants.

E. List types of air pollutants caused by the following:

   1. personal habits

   2. industry

   3. motor vehicles

   4. agriculture-pesticides

F. Define the following terms:

   1. photochemical

   2. temperature inversion

   3. smog

   4. acid rain

   5. Greenhouse Effect

   6. catalytic converter

   7. ozone layer

   8. particulate

   9. water vapor

3

DOMESTIC WATER

1. What is the source of your community's drinking water?

2. How is water treated to make it safe for drinking?

3. How many gallons of water do you use in an average day? _____

    in an average week? _____

4. What are **point** and **nonpoint** sources of water pollution?

5. Why is it easier to clean-up a river than it is to clean-up a lake?

6. List three human activities that contribute to flooding.

    1.

    2.

    3.

7. List three environmental disadvantages of building dams for water storage (reservoirs.)

8. List four types of water pollution and at least one of the sources which creates it.

9. Define the following terms:

   a. **Biological Oxygen Demand (BOD)**

   b. **aquifer**

   c. **water table**

   d. **hydrologic cycle**

4
SOIL RESOURCES

Name_____

1. List and briefly describe the major methods for reducing soil erosion and the depletion of nutrients in topsoil.

2. How can ground water become contaminated with hazardous chemicals from distant as well as local sources?

3. Briefly describe the characteristics of the different soil horizon layers listed below:

O-

A-

E-

B-

C-

R-

4. Define or explain the following terms:

   a. leaching

   b. humus

   c. physical weathering

   d. chemical weathering

   e. soil texture

   f. compost

   g. green manure

   h. salinization

5   **Name**_____

POPULATION

1. What conditions are responsible for **heavy** population concentrations?
   Explain your answer.

2. What conditions are responsible for **sparse** populations around the world?
   Explain your answer.

3. List and explain two ways by which population densities are measured.
   Give the merits and demerits of each system.

4. Are there any areas of the world that could probably support a heavier
   population density? Where are they and why do you think so?

5. Why do the main population concentrations tend to be on the continent margins and the sparse populations in the interiors?

6. Which countries have the highest percentage of urban population? List at least five.

7. List and briefly explain five factors which influence parents to have large families.

8. What is meant by a rural population? List at least five countries which have a predominantly rural population.

Name_____

USING POPULATIONS STATISTICS

REFER TO PAGE 43

When comparing countries it is customary to divide populations in groups of 1000. Thus, a country with a small population can be compared to one with a large population.

All countries record births and deaths. Therefore, population trends can be determined for each country and compared with others. In one comparison we use the Crude Birth Rate (CBR) and the Crude Death Rate (CDR). By subtracting the CDR from CBR we determine the population increase per 1000 people.

To find the annual population increase of a country we take the CBR minus the CDR and multiply times the number of 1000s in a given country.

EXAMPLE: Using the above data we can calculate that Japan's natural annual increase in population is 496,000 individuals.

$$11 - 7 = 4 \qquad 4 \times 124{,}000 = 496{,}000$$

We use the number 124,000 instead of 124,000,000 since we are calculating on the number of 1000s in Japan.

A. Calculate the natural increase in population for the following countries:

1. **United States**

2. **Pakistan**

3. **United Kingdom**

4. **Canada**

5. **Nigeria**

6. **Mexico**

DOUBLING TIME

It is also possible to calculate the number of years it will take a country to double its population if the data does not change appreciable over a number of years. The doubling time is calculated by dividing the percent rate of increase into 70.

EXAMPLE: Since Japan's natural increase is 4 per 1000 we divide 4 by 10 which equals .4 (the percent of the increase.) Thus Japan will double its population in 175 years.

$$70/.4 = 175$$

B. Calculate the doubling time for the countries listed below. This is the time a country needs to double its productivity social services and food supply just to maintain its present standard of living.

1. **United States**

2. **Pakistan**

3. **Brazil**

4. **Mexico**

5. **India**

6. **Egypt**

7   Name_____

CITIES

1. List in order the ten most populous cities of the world.

2. On the United states map, name and locate the ten most populous cities of the country. Shade in the area referred to a Megalopolis.

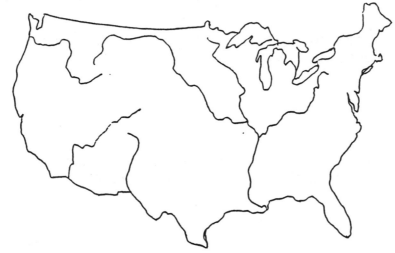

3. List five advantages of living in a city as opposed to living in a small town.

4. List five disadvantages of living in a city as opposed to living in a small town.

5. PICK CITY: **INDIANAPOLIS, INDIANA**

   a. What is the present population of our pick city?

   USE A POPULATION OF 740,000

   b. Assuming 2 people to a bedroom - how many bedrooms does it take to house this population?

   c. Assuming 160 gallons of water per person per day, how many gallons of water does the city population use in a week?

   d. Each person discards about 5 pounds of trash a day. How many tons of trash does our pick city produce in a week?

   e. Assuming two pounds of food per person per day - how much food is consumed by our pick city in the month of April?

   f. If half the population are tax paying adults and an annual per capita tax of ten dollars is levied - how much money does this produce?

   g. If half the city population is school age children and there are 25 students per class, how many classrooms must out city provide for education?

8   Name_____

MAJOR WORLD FOODS

1. List three worldwide environmental problems created by crop agriculture and state how we can decrease their impact.

2. List four minor grains and why they would be grown instead of wheat, rice, or maize.

3. Fill in the chart below with the answers required.

	WHEAT	RICE	MAIZE
Three Leading Producers			
Three Leading Exporters			
Three Leading Importers			
Major Climate Association			

4. List the nine major meat animals of the world used as food.
   List two countries that produce each in large numbers.

5. List four commercial products we get from animals other than meat.

6. If we used grain for human food instead of feeding it to animals we could
   feed about a third more people in the world so why not do it? Your
   opinion.

7. List four environmental problems created by raising animals for food.

9   Name_____

RANGE LANDS

1. On the world map:
   a. delineate and shade in the major areas of steppe vegetation.
   b. delineate and dot in major areas of savanna vegetation.

2. Define the following terms as they apply to rangeland plant species.

   a. **decreaser-**

   b. **increaser-**

   c. **invader-**

3. List the three leading countries in the production of the following animals.

   a. **cattle-**

   b. **sheep-**

   c. **goats-**

4. Why did question 3 not include swine?

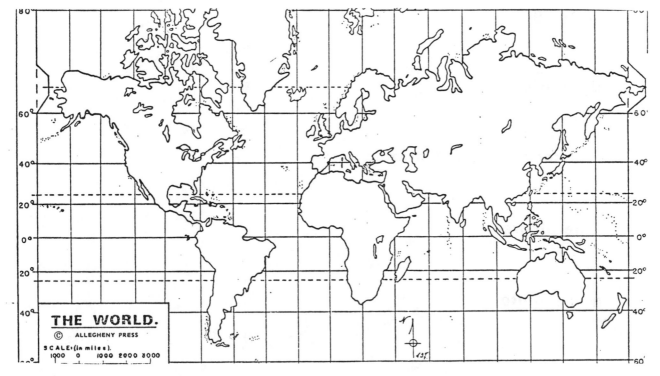

5. By what methods are the following animal groups controlled on rangelands?

    a. **rodents-**

    b. **predators-**

6. Briefly explain the duties of the U.S. Bureau of Land Management.

7. Briefly define or explain the following terms:

    a. **ruminant-**

    b. **rangeland carrying capacity-**

    c. **overgrazing-**

    d. **prairie-**

    e. **deferred rotation grazing-**

    f. **herbivore-**

    g. **mesquite-**

10

Name_____

FORESTS

1. On the United States map, draw in the approximate boundaries and label the location of the following natural vegetation zones.

   a. Northern Evergreens
   b. Central Hardwoods
   c. Southern Pine
   d. Northwest Fir and Spruce
   e. Redwoods
   f. Rocky Mountain Ponderosa

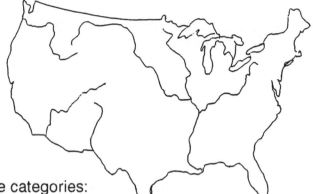

2. List three tree species for each of the categories:

   a. shade intolerant-

   b. shade tolerant-

   c. moderately shade tolerant-

3. List four tree diseases and their causes.

4. List four insects that attack trees and their tree specie preference.

5. Briefly explain the value of tropical rainforests to the rest of the world.

6. List at least four conservation methods or life-style changes that would help preserve our forests.

7. Define or explain the following as they pertain to forests:

   a. **clear cutting-**

   b. **selective cutting-**

   c. **coppicing-**

   d. **crown fire-**

11

Name_____

WILDLIFE: PLANTS AND ANIMALS

1. List at least three human activities which cause wildlife species to become
   endangered or extinct.

2. Why should we try to preserve all wildlife species?

3. Should we try to control predators in a natural wild habitat? Why or why not?

4. How is the pet trade destructive to wildlife?

5. Should we use animals for medical research? Briefly defend your answer.

6. List four factors which deplete waterfowl populations.

7. Briefly list and explaining four essential habitat requirements of wildlife.

8. How do "Game Laws" protect endangered or threatened species?

9. In your opinion - Is it ethical to manipulate nature? Give some support to your answer.

12   Name_____

RESOURCES OF THE SEA

1. List the six countries of the world that have the largest tonnage of fish caught annually. List the most important type of fish caught by each.

2. After the following headings list the animal life of the sea that are of commercial value. If it is a non-food item, list its product.

    a.   **mollusks-**

    b.   **crustaceans-**

    c.   **fish-**

    d.   **reptiles-**

    e.   **mammals-**

3. What is "fish meal" and what are its main uses?

4. Briefly describe the following methods of fishing.

    a. snaring-

    b. drift nets-

    c. seining-

    d. trawling-

    e. weir-

    f. harpooning-

    g. bait fishing-

5. List three types of sea plants that are used commercially.

6. What are the major pollutants put into the oceans by the following activities or entities?

    a. municipalities-

    b. industry-

    c. agriculture-

    d. fishing industry-

    e. resort areas-

Name_____

FUELS

1. List the factors which determine whether or not a coal seam will be mined.

2. Where are the major United States coal fields located?

3. List the major oil fields of the United States.

4. What are oil shales?

5. List four large countries which have little or no petroleum reserves.

6. List the four countries leading in petroleum reserves.

    Three leaders in coal reserves.

7. What elements form natural gas?

8. List the three leading countries in natural gas reserves.

9. Where are the major United States gas reserves located?

10. What are some alternate sources of gas for industrial and domestic uses?

11. List the major environmental problems created by the following activities and some steps to be taken to alleviate these problems.

   a. **coal mining**

   b. **coal burning**

   c. **oil drilling**

d. oil transportation

e. oil product usage

f. natural gas production

g. cutting wood for fuel

h. wood burning

FILL IN THE CHART WITH THE ANSWERS REQUIRED.

	COAL	PETROLEUM	NATURAL GAS
Major Producing Countries			
Major Consuming Countries			
Principal uses of the Fuel			
Methods of Transport			
Advantages of the Fuel			
Disadvantages of the Fuel			

14

Name_____

HAZARDOUS AND NUCLEAR WASTES

The federal government has basic siting regulations for hazardous waste landfills.
The sketch (cross section) illustrates a landfill conforming to these requirements.

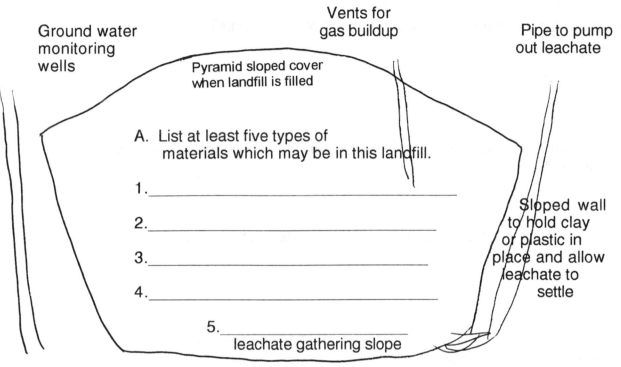

Ground water monitoring wells

Vents for gas buildup

Pipe to pump out leachate

Pyramid sloped cover when landfill is filled

A. List at least five types of materials which may be in this landfill.

1._____

2._____

3._____

4._____

5._____
leachate gathering slope

Sloped wall to hold clay or plastic in place and allow leachate to settle

B. List at least five possible events which may occur to make this type of landfill inoperable or a threat to human welfare.

C. Is it legal to put radioactive materials into hazardous waste landfills? Explain your answer.

D. NUCLEAR ENERGY

1. What happens to the radioactive wastes created by nuclear power plants?

2. What are the radioactive waste products of nuclear plants?

3. What other industries besides nuclear power plants produce radioactive wastes?

4. How long will wastes generated by nuclear power plants remain radioactive?

5. Besides radioactive wastes, how else do nuclear power plants create undesirable environmental effects?

6. What are some benefits of nuclear power?

15

Name_____

REVIEW OF A NEWSPAPER ARTICLE

The latest events concerning the environment and conservation are reported daily through television and the newspaper. Since a television broadcast is a fleeting entity while newspapers are easier to preserve you are asked to review a newspaper article.

A. Select a recent newspaper article dealing with conservation of the environment and answer the following questions.

    1. What is the headline on the article?

    2. What city and state is given in the dateline?

    3. What newspaper printed the article?

    4. On what date did the article appear?

    5. What is the source of the information of the article?
       That is, who says that information is correct?

6. Is there some way to check and verify the facts given in the article? How could you do this?

7. On the other side, briefly summarize the gist of the article.